D1602315

WORDS &C

FIRST INDIAN: *"Why single column?"*
SECOND INDIAN: *"Chief Running Fox is on another blanket.*
We're on hold."

WORDS &C

JOHN F. GUMMERE

ILLUSTRATIONS BY BEN WOLF

Edited by Jean Barth Toll
Designed by Adrianne Onderdonk Dudden

Contents

PART FOUR   UNRULY GRAMMAR

PART FIVE   MEANING, MESSAGE, AND METAPHOR

PART SIX FUN WITH WORDS

Foreword

Jack Gummere speaks! In these pages we hear his voice for all time through a medium he loved and greatly respected—the printed word.

"Pragmatic, shrewd, coolly reserved, brimming over always with life and witticisms stored in his learned head" was the way Lawrence Miller Ryle, former student and lifelong friend, described him. To this I would add that he had bounce, verve, energy, and brilliance, that he was as robust in his approach to language as to life. I don't feel he would mind being compared with his passion for language to Billy Sunday's approach to religion—through the medium of baseball. Jack Gummere and Billy Sunday were both American originals.

Jack's rapid and surefire speech indicated a quick, active mind. There was nothing passive about him, whether he was approaching life or language. And language was his life.

Jack Gummere's world was the world of academe: those who studied with him were the fortunate ones; those who did not were aware of their loss. In this book, *Words &c*, he makes it immediately apparent how fascinating the study of language is, can be.

His teaching was legendary during his lifetime and will always be so as his students pass on his wisdom to future generations. M. Albert Linton, Jr., mathematics teacher at the William Penn Charter School, wrote: "Jack believed that good teaching was the most important ingredient for a good school, and he never deviated from his firm commitment to seek good teachers who were themselves committed to excellence in the classroom."

John Flagg Gummere was born in Swarthmore, Pennsylvania, on July 27, 1901, and was a graduate of the William Penn Charter School (1918). He received his A.B. degree in 1922 from Haverford

College, where his great-great grandfather had been head. In 1933 he received his Ph.D. in Indo-European languages from the University of Pennsylvania. His life before, during, and after his graduation from the university was devoted to teaching: first at West Philadelphia High School, later at Penn Charter, where he was headmaster for twenty-seven years, and finally, at Haverford College, where he was a lecturer in the classics and humanities. He was a member of the Board of Managers of the college for thirty-eight years and served as secretary of the College Corporation.

Along with his record as an educator, he left the legacy we find in *Words &c,* the title of his column in the *Philadelphia Inquirer.* His frame references range from Yogi Berra to John Steinbeck to Ann Bridge to the fathers of language, be they Greek, Latin, or otherwise. He speaks of melody, intonation, meaning, and diction as well as etymology. Those who listened to Jack in life know to what a fine art he elevated conversation.

In our midst sat a sage. This is his testament.

John Francis Marion

Acknowledgments

The Gummere family is extremely grateful to Jean Barth Toll for her time and expertise as editor of *Words &c* and to the following people for their assistance in checking references in the manuscript: Howard Comfort, professor of classics, emeritus, Haverford College; Joanne Hutchinson, associate professor of English, Haverford College; Oscar E. Jansson, business manager (retired), William Penn Charter School; Fritz Kempner, teacher of classics and German (retired), William Penn Charter School; Joseph Russo, professor of classics, Haverford College; Edward O. Shakespeare, teacher of English (retired), Shipley School; Richard R. Smith, teacher of French and Italian, William Penn Charter School; and staff members of the Haverford College Library. Attorney/author Alan W. Armstrong encouraged the publication of *Words &c* over the years. Staff members of the Haverford College Computer Center and Central Services gave useful technical advice for producing the book.

The Contributors

BEN WOLF, whose drawings illustrate the author's captions, is a man of great diversity: an artist, editor, poet, teacher, critic, and lecturer. His art work has been exhibited in Philadelphia at the Pennsylvania Academy of the Fine Arts, the Philadelphia Art Alliance, and the Newman Galleries, and nationwide in Santa Barbara, Santa Fe, Minneapolis, Indianapolis, New York, and Provincetown.

He is the author of biographies of the artists Morton L. Schamberg, Franklin Watkins, and Harold Weston, and of a volume of poetry, *A Common of Piscary*. He has another collection of poems and a book of childhood memories in preparation. As a critic, he has been a member of the staffs of *Art Digest* and *Philadelphia Art News* and a contributor to *Art in America*, *Horizon*, the *New Mexico Quarterly*, and the *National Observer*.

JOHN FRANCIS MARION, who contributed the foreword, has devoted himself to writing and lecturing in Philadelphia since 1972; he has been an editor and a literary agent. His work includes *Lucrezia Bori of the Metropolitan Opera*, *The Charlestown Story*, and *Famous and Curious Cemeteries*. The Athenaeum of Philadelphia honored the last work in 1979, naming it the "outstanding work of non-fiction" by a Philadelphian published the previous year. His books on Philadelphia subjects include *Within These Walls*, a history of the first 125 years of the Academy of Music in Philadelphia, *Philadelphia Medica*, and *Walking Tours of Historic Philadelphia*, called "the most elegantly written Philadelphia guidebook of all time."

PART I
THE WORLD OF LANGUAGE

1
Word Geography

"I knowed you wasn't Oklahomy folks. You talk queer, kinda—that ain't no blame, you understan."

"Everybody says words different," said Ivy. "Arkansas folks says 'em different, and Oklahomy folks says 'em different. And we seen a lady from Massachusetts, she said 'em differentest of all. Couldn't hardly make out what she was sayin."*

People do, indeed, say 'em different, and it must be said, first and foremost, that it "ain't no blame." Differences, oddities, illogicalities, ridiculous idioms, strange noises, and many ways of signaling meaning, *all* are discussed here and offered for entertainment. For language is entertaining. Yogi Berra said that you can see a lot just by looking. You can also hear a lot just by listening. We propose to look and listen. "All the world's a stage" to do so.

A convenient way of looking and listening to differences is through word geography; we use the Eastern United States here as a laboratory. People from a variety of areas settled various parts of the East Coast at various times. Each group brought its own special vocabulary, homely words that have persisted in use down to the present date. Researchers seek out informants, especially those in rural areas where urbanization has not yet leveled usage.

Figure 2 gives the rough outlines of the several speech areas of the East Coast. Area (1), Eastern New England, has *teeter totter* (seesaw). Area (2), the Hudson Valley, has *pot cheese* (cottage cheese). In area (3), the Philadelphia area, we may hear *buttonwood* (sycamore). Area (4) is the Pennsylvania German area where we

*John Steinbeck, *The Grapes of Wrath* (New York: Viking Press, 1939), 184.

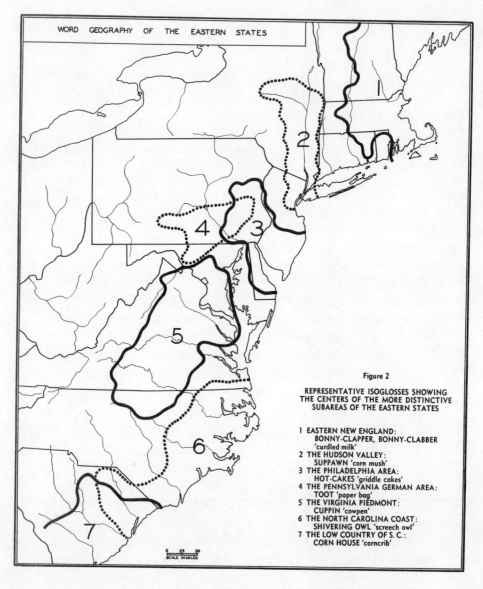

WORD GEOGRAPHY OF THE EASTERN STATES

Figure 2

REPRESENTATIVE ISOGLOSSES SHOWING
THE CENTERS OF THE MORE DISTINCTIVE
SUBAREAS OF THE EASTERN STATES

1 EASTERN NEW ENGLAND:
   BONNY-CLAPPER, BONNY-CLABBER
   'curdled milk'
2 THE HUDSON VALLEY:
   SUPPAWN 'corn mush'
3 THE PHILADELPHIA AREA:
   HOT-CAKES 'griddle cakes'
4 THE PENNSYLVANIA GERMAN AREA:
   TOOT 'paper bag'
5 THE VIRGINIA PIEDMONT:
   CUPPIN 'cowpen'
6 THE NORTH CAROLINA COAST:
   SHIVERING OWL 'screech owl'
7 THE LOW COUNTRY OF S. C.:
   CORN HOUSE 'corncrib'

0   25   50
SCALE IN MILES

SOURCE: Hans Kurath, *A Word Geography of the Eastern United States* (Ann Arbor: University of Michigan Press, 1949).

hear *ponhaus* (Philadelphia scrapple). Area (5), Virginia Piedmont, has *snake doctor* (dragon fly). Area (6), the North Carolina Coast, has *slam across* (clear across). In area (7), South Carolina Low Country, a cow may *hum* (moo). Other typical words are cited in the illustration. In each instance the words describe ordinary household words, terms that people grew up with, terms that no teacher fussily criticized as "wrong." For all are "correct," each in its own area.

In any group, a discussion of such terms leads to a discovery of a surprising assortment of individual vocabularies. A good term to try is *dragon fly*. In area (1) it is a *devil's darning needle*, and it is a *snake feeder* in many places in Pennsylvania. Someone may call it a *spindle*. Did that come from the southern tip of New Jersey or somewhere in that area? *Seesaw* may be the most common term for that piece of playground equipment, but on Cape Cod it may be a *tilt* or a *tilting board* (surely a logical name), whereas one may hear on Block Island the cheeriest of names, *tippity bounce*.

Prepositions vary. What word is used to fill in the blank in "It's a quarter —— ten" to describe 9:45 A.M.? We may hear *to, of, before,* and *till*. What word is used for the blank in "He ate something that disagreed with him, so he was sick —— his stomach." People use *at, in, on,* and *to.*

In areas (3) to (7) we hear *bucket*, not *pail*. Jack and Jill would go up that hill to get a *bucket* of water. We commonly use *fetch* when training a dog (to fetch and carry). However, it has a different meaning from *bring*. A messenger *goes* somewhere to *fetch* an object. A messenger *comes* from somewhere with an object. A fine, homely term is *earthworm*, which may be an *angle worm*, area (1); *red worm*, area (6); *ground worm*, area (5); or *rain worm*, area (3). In some places a frying pan is a *skillet*, and a *gunny sack* is a *croker sack*. Some people call a chipmunk a *grinnie*. The *creek* of Pennsylvania is a *brook* when we get as far north as Bound Brook, New Jersey. Naturally, geographical features determine speech areas. Coastal areas often tend to retain special terms. Thus we find *earthworm* in the Buzzard's Bay area of Massachusetts, and on Nantucket Island a bull may be a *masculine*.

But a mobile population, and the leveling influence of a generally better educated public, plus universal TV, tend to drive out local usages. What a pity if we lose such splendid words as may be heard for the screech owl (*Otus asio*), the only owl that has tufted ears: *squich owl* (Virginia), *squinch owl* (Maryland), *scrooch owl* (the Carolinas), and *shivering owl* (North Carolina Coast). The fine old art of coasting downhill on a sled seems to be itself going downhill. Ask those who have enjoyed it whether they called a certain position a *belly flop, belly whacker, belly buster, belly womper*, or *belly grinder*.

Hans Kurath's *A Word Geography of the United States* discusses this subject fully.*

2
We Learn to Speak by Listening

Every language has its own unique set of sounds, its sound pattern, and its own unique structure. Yet any ordinary child learns them both without benefit of text or teacher. Learning is by ear.

So remarkable is the human brain that whether the native tongue be Urdu or Finnish, Hindi or Portuguese, the child manages to sort out the sounds in the surrounding torrent of speech, makes sense of them, puts them together into words, and puts words together to form grammatically correct utterances. It does not matter how astonishingly different one sound pattern may be from another, or how radically the structures vary. The child learns them at a very early age in accordance with the native tongue.

The child needs no phonetician to imitate the surrounding

---

* All publications referred to in the text are cited in the Bibliography.

sounds or explain how they are produced. For example, the first consonants of English *Rome*, of French *Rome*, of Italian *Roma*, are all different and must be produced in different ways. Yet nobody needs to make sure the young child "does it right." The child somehow finds out how to do it right. As to structure, the native speaker of English discovers that in "Cat sees dog" the doer of the act comes first, and the meaning is reversed when one says, "Dog sees cat." This is a cardinal principle of English grammar, learned, once more, with no text or teacher. In an inflected language, such as Latin, the first word may not be the subject.

Thus the native-born illiterate (meaning someone who cannot read or write) learns to manage the language very well indeed and at the same early age. A child of three will be a fluent speaker, and reading or writing has nothing to do with the case. Moreover, the choice of *doesn't* instead of *don't*, or *isn't* for *ain't* has to do with sociology, not the production of idiomatic speech, and belongs to sociolinguistics, not to grammar.

Few of us can ever learn to speak another language as well as the native-born illiterate, unless we, too, learn it at a very early age. For language involves all sorts of sounds, many of which we must acquire (for example, the vowel in French *tu*). Besides sounds, we must acquire the intonation pattern. In our English grammar, for instance, we hear four levels of pitch, and four levels of stress, all of which have meaning (W. Nelson Francis, *Structure of American English*).

Furthermore, the majority of the three thousand languages spoken on earth have never been written down. Vocabularies may be limited, but that is a matter of lexicography, not of grammar. The speakers have all the terms they need; and if they need a new one, they will add it, probably using the name given it by those from whom it comes; or they can make up their own.

It is important to speak in such a way as to secure maximum cooperation from those with whom we come in contact. Some students have been taught to speak "Parisian French" not because the sounds it contains are of themselves any "better" than the sounds of any other dialect of French. The value of this dialect is that traditionally it has been the dialect of the people who have the influence, the education, the prestige.

3
The Indo-European Languages

Scholars believe that a group of people must have lived for a considerable length of time somewhere near the Europe-Asia border, because their language was so well developed that they took it with them when they migrated into Western Europe, Persia, and India. Words for common things found in each of these areas clearly relate to those in the others.

The Indic branch includes several languages spoken in the Indian subcontinent, the most ancient being Sanskrit. The Balto-Slavic branch includes Russian, Polish, Czechoslovak, Lithuanian, and Bulgarian. The Germanic branch includes the Scandinavian tongues, English, German, Dutch, and Flemish. The Celtic has Welsh, Breton, Irish, and Gaelic. The Italic branch had several dialects (Umbrian, Oscan, and others), but the might of Rome caused them all to disappear and Latin to prevail, though Greek continues in its peninsula today.

In these branches we find various forms of the same words for various items such as the horse or the beech tree. The root seen in the Greek word for "snow" is the same as that in the Latin word for "winter." So we can conclude that the Indo-Europeans must have come from an area that got cold. We find related words for "plow" and "mill" and "grind," giving a clue to their culture. They used the decimal system for counting—logical for creatures with ten fingers. But some cultures had a vigesimal system, counting by twenties. Did these people use fingers and toes in counting?

Pioneers in the study of Indo-European languages were the brothers Grimm, Jacob and Wilhelm, to whom we owe the folk tales. Observing the similarities of words in the various branches of Indo-European, they drew up an elementary table of correspondence of consonants. The following table is commonly used to illustrate this correspondence:

English:	seven	ten	father
Greek:	hepta	deka	pater
Latin:	septem	decem	pater
Lithuanian:	septyni	deszimt	[NA]
Sanskrit:	sapta	daca	pita

One can see that English has /f/ and /t/ where Latin and Greek have /p/ and /d/.

To show a much closer correspondence, we list the later form of Latin words in areas into which Latin-speaking people penetrated, imposing Latin on the local populace. Just as is the case with Indo-European, we find regional variations. Classical Latin changed over the centuries, and local developments were furthered by the isolation and lack of communication among such areas as are now called Spain, France, Italy, Romania, Portugal, and Provence (the southern part of France). The fall of the Roman Empire thus produced a number of neo-Latin languages. Because the declensions of Latin, in which the endings of words signaled meaning, disappeared and prepositions replaced them, the accusative case became generalized, and so is the source of most nouns in the Romanic languages. Here is a table that shows the relationships:

Latin:	septem	decem	patrem
Italian:	sette	dieci	padre
French:	sept	dix	père
Portuguese:	sete	dez	padre
Provencal:	set	detz	paire
Romanian:	septe	diece	[NA]
Spanish:	siete	diez	padre

In Indo-European families, English and German are cousins, so to speak, and we can find consonant relationships between them.

German words beginning in *Z* appear in their English cognates with *T*: *Zug/tug; zu/to; zehn/ten. T* turns up as *D*: *Tor/door; trag-en/drag; Tal/dale. D* is *TH*: *dank-en/thank; denk-en/think; Dieb/thief.*

Two distant cousins (cognates), now residing far apart, are Germanic (to which group English belongs) and Latin (of the Italic group). Latin *T* may appear as *TH*: *tres/three; tu/thou; ton-are/thunder; tum-or/thumb* (the thumb is the protruding part of the hand). *C* (= *K*) corresponds to *H*: *coll-is/hill; caput/head. Corn-u/horn* refers to a growth on an animal's head or a growth on a human's toe; also to musical instruments made from the horns of animals.

It is surprising to find a number of Sanskrit words (from the Indic family) corresponding to their Latin cognates: *nom-en/nam-a,* (name in English); *voc-em/vac-am* (voice). Latin *mag* (big) is *mah* in Sanskrit; and Latin *reg* (king) is Sanskrit *raj.* Thus *maharajah* means "big king." Latin *duo* (two) is Sanskrit *dva.*

Finnish, Turkish, and Hungarian, by the way, though they are spoken in the "Indo-European area," have no connection.

There have been a number of efforts to create a "universal" language, notably Esperanto. But the sounds and structure of other languages are so radically different from ours and from one another that the only practical thing to do is to adopt English, which is already the leading *lingua franca* of the business world.

PART TWO
LISTENING TO LANGUAGE

4
The Sounds of English

Each language has its own unique set of sounds (sound pattern) which the native speaker learns, as mentioned earlier, by ear at a very early age. There is no need to analyze the sounds or list them because they "come naturally." Yet anyone interested in language could find out just what these sounds are, describe them, and list them.

As we are accustomed to our own sounds, other languages sound "funny" to us. What is funny or strange comes to be thought of as odd. Odd implies inferior. So the Greeks, imitating what they thought were the sounds of "foreign" languages, described the speakers as *barbaroi*, that is, "babblers." Whence comes our word *barbarian*. This sort of prejudice is almost automatic. Ann Bridge, in one of her fine novels, succumbs to this attitude when she describes one character: "He *gabbled* something in Portuguese." Other people *gabble*; we *speak*. But what about a language that expects one to get around such words as *sixths*, or *twelfths*, or *strengths*, each of which ends in a cluster of four consonants? We can even manage "thou triumphst," which also ends in four (not five) consonants.

Long ago, linguistic scholars warned against trying to describe a language by means of writing. There is no set of ink marks ever devised that can adequately represent sounds. The analysis made by Edward Sapir of a number of American Indian languages that had never been written down pointed up this important fact. Indeed, as must repeatedly be emphasized, most languages spoken on earth have never been written down.

The total number of consonants in English cannot be discovered from ink marks on a page, especially the spelling of English.

We use two letters to represent some consonants (three for one of them) and we spell consonants in different ways.

Here, then is our list. Note that we have eight pairs that differ only in whether a sound is voiceless (the vocal cords do not vibrate) or voiced (vocal cords vibrate). Phonetic symbols are shown for each consonant:

Voiceless:	hit	cap	back	hiss	fine	rich	ash	ether
Phonetic symbol:	/t/	/p/	/k/	/s/	/f/	/č/	/š/	/θ/
Number:	1	3	5	7	9	11	13	15
Voiced:	hid	cab	bag	his	vine	ridge	azure	either
Phonetic symbol:	/d/	/b/	/g/	/z/	/v/	/ǰ/	/ž/	/ð/
Number:	2	4	6	8	10	12	14	16

There are two so-called liquids, heard in *lip* /l/ and *rip* /r/ that we number, respectively, #17 and #18. There are three nasals: *rum* /m/ #19, *run* /n/ #20, and *rung* /ŋ/ #21. The third of these is called "agma" and is spelled with N alone in, for example, *rink*. Add to these: *hue* /h/ #22, *woo* /w/ #23, and *you* /y/ #24.

The following sentence, used with the permission of *American Speech* (University of Alabama Press, 1983), in which I first published it, contains a representation of each consonant (with no repeats). The letters that represent a consonant are numbered to correspond with the table above. First, the sentence:

"Sure, we five blame young Chuck: his decision to jog the path."

Now expanded to include the key numbers:

```
  S   u   r   e       w   e       f   i   v   e       b   l   a   m   e
  13      18          23          9       10          4   17      19

  y   o   u   ng  Ch  u   ck:     h   i   s       d   e   c   i   s   i   o   n
  24          21  11      5       22      8       2       7       14          20

  t   o       j   o   g       th  e       p   a   th.
  1           12      6       16          3       15.
```

This sentence may be called a "panphone," because it contains representations of all (*pan*) consonant sounds (*phones*). I claim credit for inventing this neologism, for I did not find it in the *New English Dictionary* (or its 1982 *Supplement*). Once more, we are concerned with, not consonants, but the representation of the sounds.

The initial consonants of English *ton, done,* and *none* are formed with the tongue against the ridge of the upper teeth. This is not the case with French *ton, don,* and *non,* in which the tongue is behind the upper teeth. What is of particular interest is that the native speaker in each language somehow arranges to put the tongue in the right place. No text or teacher explains or describes this matter to a three-year-old who simply does it correctly.

Similarly, the initial consonant of English *pit* is followed by a puff of breath; the same is true of *ton.* This is not true of those same consonants in *spin* and *stun.* In French, there is no puff (aspiration) after the initial consonants of *près* and *très.* Somehow, the child does the right thing, again without any instructions.

5
How to Spell a Consonant

We make fun of the weird spelling of words: "Though tired, the tough pig ploughed through the trough." But consonant spelling, sometimes using more than one letter to spell a consonant, may also be weird. Yet spelling has nothing to do with the *language,* because the language is sound, not ink marks on a page.

Consonant #12 /ǰ/ is spelled in three different ways in "Judge a gem." On the other hand, the letter *G* stands for three different consonants in "Give Gina rouge" (#6, #12, and #14).

There is an odd thing about the /z/ of *azure.* It never stands first or last in an English word. In borrowings from French, such as *garage, sabotage, prestige*, we have to learn to put it there. It is a "non-English" position. That same sound seems to be a kind of "z-like" sound. But it is represented by a Z in only seven English words: *azure, brazier* (which counts twice as meaning either a pot to hold incense or someone who works in brass), *crozier* (which is also spelled with an *S*), *glazier, grazier* (British, one who grazes cattle), and *seizure*. We generally use an *S* as in *measure* and *treasure*. In *bijou* we simply keep the French spelling. In the following sentence, *S* is used to represent four different consonants: "This is a measure of sugar."

As to the nasal "agma" /ŋ/, it is spelled with two letters in si*ng*, but with only one in si*nk*. The word *sing* does not "end in /g/" and so no one can be said to "drop a *G*" when saying *runnin'*. Incidentally, agma never begins an English word. What happens when *N* and *G* come together in spelling? In *singer*, they represent a single consonant, agma /ŋ/. In *finger*, they represent /ŋ/ plus /g/; in *danger*, /n/ plus /ǰ/.

In *sure, sugar*, and sometimes in *sumac*, *S* represents the consonant /š/. But that consonant is represented elsewhere by *SS*, as in *mission*, or by *C* in *coercion*, or by *T* in *motion*.

The consonant /f/ is represented in various ways: *fig, rough, phone, cliff*. Oddly enough, the letter *F* represents /v/ in *of*.

We sometimes write a letter twice to indicate that the vowel that precedes is short: *filling, written*. In *filing* and *writing*, the preceding sound is a diphthong (fayliŋ), (raytiŋ).

If we use that useless letter *Q* to spell anything, we always write a *U* after it. The *U* generally represents the consonant /w/ (often not suspected in *guava, persuade, suede*). Sometimes the *U* represents nothing phonetic as in *gauge, guard*.

As a grim reminder of consonant spelling, here is a list of ten ways in which we spell the consonant /k/: *acquit, back, biscuit, bisque, cat, chord, Iraq, kin, raccoon*, and *require*.

An examination of our alphabet makes us realize how inadequate and misleading it is.

6
How to Spell Vowels and Diphthongs

The sounds of vowels and diphthongs are complicated and varied in English, just as they are in any other language. Teachers in elementary schools have traditionally taught that English has five vowels. This egregious error resulted from counting the letters of the alphabet, relying, that is, on the printed word, a procedure that can *never* bring a correct result. "Miss Fidditch" *should* have said that five letters are commonly used in our efforts to represent our vowel sounds. She seems not to have discussed our abundance of diphthongs.

We hear nine short vowels in American English. Yet to represent them in writing is difficult because of the variations in dialects in the country. The following sentence yields eight short vowels in the pronunciation of a good many speakers: "Pat's jist gonna put in red pots."

Jist is a way of representing how we pronounce *just* in "unstressed" position. We reduce the sound almost to a brief utterance. The vowel is not that of *but* or that of *jest*, or that of *jib*. If we say, in some annoyance, "I *just* told you not to do that," we make it rhyme with *rust*. But if someone asks where Joe is, we reply, "I *jist* saw 'im." In other words, if the word means "only a moment ago," we hear *jist*. The vowel is represented phonetically by a small i with a bar through the middle /ɨ/, and so is often called the "barred i."

People are troubled by *gonna*, because the spelling suggests "slang" or an "uneducated" pronunciation. Yet, we all say it. The short vowel represented by the letter *O* forms a part of the diphthongs heard in *joy, boy, go, so,* in which we have a combination of sounds, the second of which may be called an "off-glide." The second vowel of *gonna* is called "schwa." It is heard at the beginning of *above* and at the end of *sofa*. (Miss Fidditch seems to have been quite unaware of the very existence of this vowel.)

The following sentence in which *A* represents five different vowel sounds is a good example of the confusion in our representation of vowel sounds: "Jack's father's called away."

The table below shows the many ways in which we try to represent the fantastic spellings of vowel sounds:

The sound as indicated in dictionaries	The spellings of these sounds in English words
ā	*say*, *break*, *eh*, *gauge*, *hate*, *they*, *vain*, *weight* (8 ways)
ē	*amoeba*, *Caesar*, *key*, *marine*, *people*, *perceive*, *quay*, *reach*, *see*, *we*, *yield* (11 ways)
ī	*aye*, *Cairo*, *eye*, *fry*, *geyser*, *guy*, *height*, *ice*, *lie*, *sigh*, *stein* (11 ways)
ō	*beau*, *bowl*, *coat*, *go*, *oh*, *owe*, *sew*, *soul*, *taupe*, *toe*, *yeoman* (11 ways)
ü	*adieu*, *beauty*, *few*, *feud*, *fuel*, *queue*, *unite*, *view*, *youth* (9 ways)
ĕ	*aesthetic*, *bury*, *friend*, *get*, *guest*, *heather*, *heifer*, *jeopardy*, *many*, *said* (10 ways)
∂	*abacus*, *about*, *curtain*, *edible*, *history*, *often*, *serious* (7 ways)

The following jingle shows how the pronunciation of vowel sounds varies in dialects of American English. (Everyone speaks a dialect, that is, some set of sounds widely used in a certain area or areas.)

Quackers and Cheese

An astonished young fellow named Terry
Found ducks weighing cheese in a dairy.
Said he, "In a forest
I'd as soon find a florist
As quackers with cheeses to carry."

For most speakers of Midland East, this poem does not rhyme at all. The first vowel of *Terry* is that of *bet*, and the first vowel of *carry* is that of *hat*. As for *forest*, the first vowel is that of *far*, and in *florist*, it is that of *for*. Yet it is likely that a majority of American speakers will find that the poem *does* rhyme. The usual test for this sort of dialectal difference is to say, "Mary is merry because she's getting married."

Here is a convenient table of the short vowels with their phonetic symbols. The vertical columns show the area in which the vowel is formed in the vertical sense. The horizontal columns show how far forward or back they are formed in the mouth:

	Front	*Central*	*Back*
High	pit /i/	jist /ɨ/	put /u/
Mid	pet /e/	putt /ə/	gonna /o/
Low	pat /æ/	pot /a/	"New England" dog /ɔ/

Source: Adapted from W. Nelson Francis, *The Structure of American English* (New York: Ronald Press, 1958), 139.

In our speech we hear these vowels combined with other sounds to form a great variety of diphthongs. A good dictionary can provide full information.

7
Plural Noises: Hiss, Buzz, Grunt and a Buzz, or Nothing

Once again, the sounds of a language differ from the letters of the alphabet; for language is noise, not ink marks on a page.

We were taught from books and so may believe that most plurals in English are formed "by adding an *s*." (The statement should end with "-*s*," because that is the way we correctly indicate that a letter ends a word. The hyphen is required, just as it is when we refer to the beginning *s*- in the spelling of *some*.)

Let us now listen to the language and see how plurals are actually formed. As in many other languages, English usually changes or adds noises at the end of words. Thus the Hebrew plural of *seraph* is *seraphim*, and the plural signal is the sound heard in the added syllable. What sound do we add for the plural of *cat*? It can be described as a "hiss"; it is phonetically written /s/. But for *dog* we add a "buzz" /z/. As for words ending in sibilants, we add what might be described as a "grunt and a buzz": *wishes, roses*, phonetically written /əz/. (We have already mentioned the vowel sound "schwa" of this termination.) But to some plural words, notably names of living creatures, we add no plural signal: *sheep, quail*.

By listening, then, we have discovered a rule for the formation of most English plurals: "Add a hiss, a buzz, or a grunt and a buzz, or nothing at all, as the case may be."

We call these "meaning signals" *morphemes*. We describe the various plural sounds that signal the same thing as *allomorphs*. Let us note that the same set of allomorphs is heard in the extra sounds we add to present-tense verbs in the third person singular. We add a hiss /s/ in *eats*, a buzz /z/ in *runs*, a grunt and a buzz /əz/

in *wishes*. Of course these extra sounds add nothing to the under-standing of meaning, but our grammar requires it. We have traces of the extinct ending of the second person singular: "Thou seest all," and of the rare third-person ending seen in "The Lord giveth and the Lord taketh away." So-called function words such as *will, shall, can, may, might, better*, and so on add no extra sounds.

The other tense in English is the preterit, the past definite. Here, too, we often add sounds. They vary depending on whether the verb ends with a voiced sound (vocal cords vibrate) or a voice-less (cords do not vibrate). For the latter, we add /t/ as in *fix/fixed/* (fikst); for the former, /d/ as in *fill/filled/*. For such as *wish, buzz*, we add /d/. For other endings we add /əd/, as in *mend/mended*. These added sounds are true morphemes because they signal meaning.

The last thing to look for in any language is logic. Languages have peculiarities. Here are some peculiar plurals. If we have *box/boxes*, why no *ox/oxes*? The plural of *goose* is *geese*, but the plural of *moose* is not *meese*. The plural of *mouse* is *mice*, but the plural of *house* is not *hice*. Laboratories report that cloned mice are called *mouses*, a splendid and useful linguistic tour de force. The famous trio of *children, brethren, oxen* is unique in English. The poetic plu-ral, *kine*, rhyming with many words, is fading away, more's the pity. The word *penny* has two plurals, *pennies* (which come from Heaven) and *pence*, providing a nice distinction between American and British coinage.

So-called mass nouns do not have a proper plural. The plurals of such as *wine, bread, cheese* refer to kinds of wine, and so on. As to the choice between *fish* and *fishes*, a fisherman catches *fish*, but we might ask how many kinds of *fishes* are in an aquarium.

The plural of *woman* is pronounced with a change in the first vowel, but the spelling makes a change in the second even though there is no change in the pronunciation in the second. The latter is justified, because the word originally stood for "wife-man" and so the plural should be "wife-men."

There is often (and reasonable) trouble with the plurals of *alumnus* (male graduate) and *alumna* (female graduate). In Latin, we pronounce the masculine plural (alumni) to rhyme with "he" and the feminine (alumnae) with "high." But when we Anglicize these words, as we probably should because they are so much a part of our ordinary vocabulary, the masculine rhymes with "high" and the feminine with "he," exactly the reverse. The word *plural* itself means "full." Indeed, English *full* is a distant cousin of the word. So a *plenary* session is supposed to be a *full* session, and a *plenipotentiary* is *full* of power.

Criterion is a Greek neuter singular, and its plural is *criteria*, yet we have so many Latin singulars ending in *-a* that the Greek plural is often treated as a singular. Words that contribute to this problem are, for example, *tuba, alumna, aura, antenna, arena.* The Italian singular for "writing" is *graffito*; so the plural is *graffiti*.

A periodical had a difficult time some years ago with the plural of *memento mori*, "remember to die," used of some accident that reminds us that we will all die. But the first word is a singular imperative. You cannot contrive a plural to refer to a series of accidents, each of which is a reminder of death. Yet that is what the editor did: he wrote *mementi mori*. All one can do in such a situation is "cheat" and refer to each incident as a *memento mori*.

There is no reason why a language has to confine itself to singulars and plurals. Things sometimes come in pairs, and this observation is particularly true of animals. In the Indo-European language, whence came Latin and Greek, there really was a "dual" number that was used of pairs. It survived in full force in classical Greek, but only traces of it remain in Latin. Two examples have come down to us: *duo* (English "dual") "two," and *ambo* (English "ambidextrous"), "both." The Greek form of the latter is *amphi*, seen in *amphi*bious animals that live both on land and in water. *Ambigu*ous has meanings both ways, and an *amphi*theater gives views from both directions. English retains a remarkable single relic: the word *both* (which happens to be from the same root as the *-bo* in *ambo*). As one comes to think of it, *both* is quite clearly a dual, referring to neither singular nor plural.

8
Sounds: Sinister or Sweet

Many people declare that they like the sound of a certain language and dislike the sound of another, calling it "guttural" or "unpleasant." Everyone is entitled to likes and dislikes, but they are a matter of purely personal choice. We may be sure that those who speak some language someone else describes as "unpleasant" do not find it so. Personal preference can generate the clouding over of intelligent understanding. Yet features of the sound pattern of a language come to be associated with certain feelings. Each language has its own unique condition.

Here are some examples of English sounds that seem to have become associated with certain feelings, "indefinable feelings," as Professor Roman Jakobson put it. Consider words that begin with /sn/, a combination of consonants that does not occur in initial position in Latin, French, Italian, or German. Such words are likely to be sinister.

A *snort* from a bull is a warning. From a person it is often sarcastic. In a glass, it is probably pretty strong. We may *sneer* at someone, *snicker* at what someone does (or *snigger*, worse yet), and follow that with a *snub*. (Yet it is all right to *snub* a rope around a cleat—you bring it up tight.) A *sniveling* creature is repulsive (see how we use the derogatory word *creature* with it). He is the sort who might well *snitch* a TV set or *snitch* on someone. A *sneak* is ready to *snatch* something, and a bad-tempered person may be in a *snit*. The *snarl* of a dog is ominous, and in a skein of wool it is a problem; in a business matter it probably results from bad management. *Sneezes* often call for apologies, and *snores* annoy us. It appears that *snails* and *snakes* may suffer more than they should because of their names.

A *snappy* dresser overdoes it. To *snap* at anyone is to be disagreeable. A *snap* victory amounts to little, and when a rope *snaps*, we gather that it is not so good as it should be. When a life is *snuffed* out (usually said of a young life), the implication is that a promising future was lost. A pig, not a person, is supposed to have a *snout*. (The root in this word, by the way, is found in *schnozzle*, itself an unlovely word.) *Snide* remarks are sly and derogatory, and a *sniper*, if not a dangerous warrior, is a police problem, or someone who takes cheap shots at others. But *Wilson's snipe*, well-known to bird watchers, has given us a slang word for a lawyer's bill, a *snipe*. Ornithologist Roger Tory Peterson wrote it has "an extremely long, slender bill. When flushed, it makes off in a zigzag, . . . and uttering a rasping note" (*A Field Guide to the Birds* [Boston: Houghton Mifflin Co., 1947], 89). Apologies to the legal profession, but that's the way it is. A *snipe* in a gutter is a previously owned cigar. Lewis Carroll's *snark* was a terror, one not to be *sniffed* at. One who goes *sniffing* around is an obnoxious intruder. Who wants to have the *sniffles* or the *snuffles*? A dog following a trail *snuffles* along.

Yet not every /sn/ word is bad. *Snow* can be nice under certain circumstances, but when someone is *snowed*, he is being fooled. A *snack* is all right, but a minor meal. A *snifter* (technically a dram of brandy) might precede a *snooze*. *Snapper* soup is highly thought of, and *snug*, at last, escapes entirely the opprobrium of the others of its group, whether it refers to a person or to a rope made fast. *Snorkels* get their name from *snout*. We do not know the origin of *snooker* in *snooker* pool.

What about proper names spelled with /sn/ at the beginning? Is there any feeling about them? A glance at a telephone directory shows that most reflect German words that begin, not with /s/ but with /š/, which we often represent by the letters *sch*. Thus *Snyder* is for *Schneider*, "tailor," and *Snell* is for *schnell*, "quick," and *Snee* is for *Schnee*, "snow."

It is a relief to turn from unhappy initial noises to cheery ones: words that begin with /tw/. The slashes, as usual, indicate a phonetic symbol. Thus two /tuw/ is not included because it does not begin with /tw/. As so often, the spelling can be confusing.

Twelve and *twenty* are mere counting words, void of any special implication. But stars *twinkle* in the *twilight*, at once brightening our lives. A *twite* (finch) *twitters* from a *twig*, probably saying, "*twee, twee*," or perhaps "*tweet tweet*." There is not much menace in a *tweak* of the nose, not much pain in a *twinge* of the arm, and to *twit* is not to scold but to tease. In clothing, *twills* and *tweeds* are well thought of. A *twerp* is not really wicked, and a *twiddle* of the thumbs is simply futile. *Tweezers* are for delicate manipulations, and a *twirl* is graceful whether on the dance floor or on ice or in handling a baton. *Twins* have a nice name as befits them, and hearts may be *entwined* figuratively, or carved on a tree, for a happy *twain*, perhaps while a guitar is *twanged*. We get a special effect by writing "*Twixt* the Devil and the deep blue sea;" and there is no better way to start a story than "'*Twas* the night before Christmas." A *twist* of the wrist suggests deftness, such as Kipling's tubes that are *twisted* and dried. A fine word to describe the jargon and nonsense heard today is *twaddle*. *Twice*-told Tales, Hawthorne's title, must be good, and what better names for twins than Lewis Carroll's *Tweedledum* and *Tweedledee*? A rare word is *twatchel*, which means an earthworm.

The voiced counterpart of /t/ is /d/, leading us to look at words that begin with /dw/. A *dwindling dwarf* can *dwell* in a dale where he may *dwine* (waste away) after taking a *dwale* (a sleeping potion) or using *dwayberry* (belladonna). We appear to have only two proper names in this category: *Dwight* and *Dwayne*, the latter perhaps just a fancy spelling for *Duane*, the former a contraction of Dutch *DeWitt*.

As with initial /tw/, English likes the sounds of /r/ and /l/, which are somewhat poetically termed "liquid consonants." They often complement one another in successive syllables. They come "trippingly on the tongue" in such words as *curl, furl, swirl, twirl*, all of which have pleasant connotations. To *furl* a flag is not simply to fold it. A *knurl* on the handle of a tool keeps fingers from slipping, and a *gnarled* oak in a painting lends atmosphere.

There are limits to the use of these consonants. We never have the sequence /lr/, except in different syllables, as in *millrace*; and no words begin either with /l/ + /n/ or /n/ + /l/. They figure prominently in onomatopoeia, the forming of words to sound like what they refer to. We find one liquid in the first syllable and another in the second: *clamor, clatter, splatter*, and *rumble, crackle, trickle*. One can think of many others. There is a notable exception: *murmur*, which might have turned into *mulmur* or *murmul* if we had not stuck to the Latin. We have many other two-syllable words with the same sequences: *flatter, flutter, platter, brittle, crumble*. This arrangement just seems to suit speakers of English.

The two sounds cooperate in the phenomenon called "dissimilation," that is, the alteration of one or another of two similar sounds that come close together. For instance, the suffix *-alis* in Latin means "pertaining to." *Capitalis* (instead of *capitalalis*) means pertaining to a capital, and *totalis* (instead of *totalalis*) means pertaining to the total. But if an /l/ is to be heard in the stem of a word, the Latin suffix obligingly avoids another /l/, and we dissimilate by using the liquid /r/. So we have, from Latin, *military, consular*, and so on. We even change the French word *marbre*, which offends us with an /r/ in successive syllables, and make it *marble*. There is an odd example of dissimilation: In *meridian* the first element is from *medius* (middle) (English median, etc.). But Latin did not like that /d/ in successive syllables. So the first one was changed to /r/, thus disguising the etymology of our word *meridian*. We stick to our /r/ /l/ pattern in *colonel*, where we let the spelling stand, but pronounce it *kernel*.

9
Coming to an Inglorious End

Just as words that begin with /sl/ or /sn/ are mostly disagreeable, so many words that end in /id/ are sad or sorrowful. Consider *fetid, flaccid, frigid, horrid, insipid, livid, pallid, putrid, rabid, stolid, stupid, torpid, vapid.* This is, indeed, a depressing array.

A *florid* face is unhealthy; *acrid* smoke stings; a *morbid* imagination is, etymologically, "diseased," and a *tepid* recommendation is no more inspiring than a *tepid* bath. One can be *rigid* with indignation at getting a *rancid* bit of meat; but will the *timid* shopper complain? *Sordid* may describe conditions in a *squalid* neighborhood. A contract may be *in-VAL-id* and a sufferer an *IN-val-id*. The *avid* person may overdo things, and the *languid* one neglects them. A desert is *arid*; the North Pole, *gelid*. A *lurid* tale may be accompanied by *acid* sarcasm.

But a *candid* account, *lucidly* told, may make a *solid* impression, perhaps even a *vivid* one.

We have an odd lot of words ending in /ddle/ which seem often to signal ineptitude. A *waddle* is awkward. One who *fiddles* around may just *muddle* through. *Twaddle* can be dismissed with a cry of "*fiddle-faddle*." The *toddler* can just barely walk, and a *riddle* is a minor kind of puzzle. A *raddled* face may indicate a *riddled* body. *Straddling* is ungainly; and *peddling*, a low-rated enterprise. *Paddling* is low-power rowing. Less lovely, to be sure, are *piddle*, and the use of *piddling* to mean unimportant, ineffective. As to *diddle*, it may mean to cheat someone, but in a minor fashion (probably from swindling Jeremy Diddler, a character in an 1803 play by James Kenney). The be-*fuddled* person is not insane, just not quite with it. *Cuddle* and *huddle* suggest minor acts, quite the opposite of anything aggressive. Such words may be classed as middle-of-the-road types.

Another futile final noise is heard in words ending in /bble/. *Cobble*, mend shoes, seems to escape this definition, but it can also mean botch a job. Here are sixteen words ending in /bble/ suggesting things undesirable or ineptitude or ugliness: *babble, bobble, bubble, dibble, dribble, gabble, gobble, hobble, nibble, pebble, rabble, rubble, scrabble, scribble, stubble, wobble*. It would be hard to find a more pathetic collection.

The ending /ob/ seems to imply things that are unattractive. A *blob*, says the American Heritage Dictionary, is "a shapeless splotch of color." (*Splotch*, by the way, is a fine word of itself, probably a combination of *blotch* and *spot*.) A *glob* is the same thing as a *blob*. A *bob* may be a jerky motion of the head, far different from a *bow*; or it may be old-time slang for a British shilling. It also defines a short haircut (or tailcut for a horse). A *fob* is a tiny pocket in a pair of pants or a ribbon attached to a watch (which was often stowed in a *fob*), commonly called a "watch fob." But if you *fob* off something on someone, you have been cheating. To *hob nob* was originally to drink to someone. Its origin is uncertain, but the development of its meaning is not. *Hobnobbing* is engaging in close association with someone with implications of something sinister. A *knob* is an ugly protuberance; no wonder artists decorate knobs. *Knobby* knees are a distressing sight. *Mob* is short for Latin *mobile*, "movable," hence "fickle." The *mobile vulgus*, "fickle, changeable crowd," has been shortened to *mob*. *Nob*, meaning a person of wealth or standing, is used in a pejorative way. As to *rob* and *slob*, they should feel very much at home in this company.

Exceptions we always find: *job*; what is a nice word like that doing here? We have some other rather disreputable words spelled with a final vowel + /b/: *glib, flub, flab, carb, slab*. James Thurber used to enjoy making up words with odd consonant uses. Why not *Xob*, a spaceman, leader of marauders from the planet Sepsis? Or *zob*, a person who reads a newspaper and leaves it folded crooked with pages sticking out at the sides?

That *muffled* sound we hear comes from a batch of odd words.

A *bufflehead*, if not a duck, is a stupid fellow. To *riffle* the pages of a book is to pay it little attention, and to *shuffle* along is to signal sadness, someone *baffled* by life, whose feelings have been badly *ruffled*. This individual may *sniffle* as he goes on his way. None of us wants a *snaffle* in his mouth. None of us wants somebody to *waffle* in a statement (but we do like *waffles*). The same root, however, is in *weevil*. It is also in *wafer*, and shows its basic meaning in *weave*. *Trifles* may be on sale at a *raffle*. Is there a good red-blooded word in the lot, with a good, solid, positive meaning?

We cannot admit *duffle* (*duffel*) because it comes from the name of the town, Duffel, in Belgium. But we do admit that most of the words in this collection have about as much punch to them as *piffle*.

10
A Collection of
Oddities and Curiosities

Every language has its oddities. For instance, here are three English words, each spelled with nine letters, and yet they contain only one vowel sound: *broughams, straights, strengths*. The first word is commonly pronounced as a homonym of *brooms*. We ought to note another oddity: in *strengths*, we hear a /k/, as we do in *lengths*.

The detachment of the final -*n* of *an* is seen in *an ewt* turning into *a newt*. *Ewt*, by the way, is from the same root as *eft*, that handy word for crossword puzzles. The transfer of an initial *n-* of a word back to the article is seen in what used to be *a napron* and is now *an apron*. The *n-* is still in place in related words such as *napery* and *napkin*. *An adder* was originally *a nadder*, and a *non-par*,

that is *a numpire* is now *an umpire*. We can assume that *non-par*
implied "not on either side."

We are not fond of words that end in *-sp*, having a round
dozen: *asp, clasp, crisp, cusp, gasp, grasp, hasp, knosp* (a knob), *lisp,
rasp, wasp, wisp*. (This list makes a good trivia question.)

Other languages have initial consonant combinations that are
not heard in English. Greek *pterodactyl* (wing finger), *psychology*;
Italian *sbagliare* (make a mistake), in which the first consonant is
/z/, as it is in *smarrire* (lose). It comes as a surprise to speakers of
English to realize that we do not end words with /h/, though we
often write the letter *H* on the end of a word (*hurrah*, for example).
Perhaps we do produce a puff of breath in the exclamations *huh*
and *hah* (cry of triumph). Observe that words spelled with *T + H*
on the end have only one consonant there; we use two letters to
represent that consonant /th/. French begins words with /ž/, the
consonant we represent by a *Z* in *seizure*.

In spite of the confusion caused by homonyms with their different meanings, English keeps a good many. Only the context distinguishes them. Trios are the interesting ones: *cite, sight, site*. There
is the well-known triple pun: "When a father left his cattle ranch to
his male offspring, it was called 'Focus.' That is where the *sun's rays
meet*, or the *sons raise meat*."

Bow /aw/ (front of a ship or a bend at the waist) is a homo-
graph (identical spelling), and may be pronounced differently as in
bow /ow/ (knot in a tie or a device for shooting arrows or for playing a violin).

Regional pronunciations enter into a group of four: *air, ere, heir,*
and *err*. The last one is not a homonym in the speech of many
Americans, especially those on the East Coast, where it rhymes
with *burr*. A homonym of *raise* is *raze*. If we are referring to build-
ings, they are antonyms.

The following riddle involves an oddity of spelling:

I know a word of plural number
A bar to peace and human slumber.
But adding *S* to this,

How strange a metamorphosis!
Plural is plural no more,
Sweet is what was bitter before.

(The answer is given at the end of the chapter.)

Words are likely to be shortened and changed as they pass through generations of speakers. A remarkable example of a collapse of syllables is the development from two Latin words:

Latin:	*mea domina* "my lady"	(five syllables)
Italian:	*madonna*	(three syllables)
French:	*madame*	(two syllables)
English:	*madam*	(six letters to five)
English:	*m'am*	(one syllable)
English:	*yes'm*	(a vocalic consonant)

Since homonyms and homographs are distinguished only by the context in which they are found, the lexicographer has to study those contexts, usually quoting from some author. But what is to be done when a word occurs only once? The Greek word in the Lord's Prayer that is commonly translated *daily* ("Give us this day our *daily* bread") embodies this problem. It is not found anywhere else in all the Greek we know of. We know the elements that compose it, but that is not enough. What we have is simply an educated guess.

Q is a "pequliar" letter. In our orthography it occurs only with the letter U following. We got it, like the rest of the alphabet, from the Phoenicians, via the Etruscans, via the Romans. The Greeks abandoned it, for they did not need it any more than we need it (K serves its purpose). It would be simpler to write *kwik* for "quick." Anyway, the Phoenicians called the letter "*qoph*."

When Arabic is written in the Roman alphabet, Q is used to represent a consonant we do not have in English. We cannot pronounce *Quatar* or *Qum* correctly without special instruction and practice. It happens that *qoph* means "monkey." The letter was shaped like a circle with a vertical diameter extending a bit below the rim of the circle. The Romans curled that extension to the right, thus putting a tail on the monkey: Q.

Other languages, like English, have a written U after a Q, but it does not represent a sound any more than it does in English *guard*, *gauge*. For us, the U represents the consonant usually written with a W. Some interesting words are spelled with a Q: *quarks* (objects that may be the basic building matter of everything); *quoin* (the corner of a building). As to *quick*, it really means alive. The *quick* of a fingernail is alive and growing; a *quick* move is a lively one; and we would prefer to belong to the *quick* rather than the dead. *Quicksand* is alive and so is *quicklime*; and a good name for mercury, which slips quickly away, is *quicksilver*.

Sometimes a Q has a special appeal that leads to error:

A Q looks cute in barbeque.
Alas, alack! It will not do.
What loss of glamourosity;
We're s'pozed to spell it with a C!

(Answer to the riddle: *cares/caress*. Similar changes are seen in *bustle/bustless*, and *rustle/rustless*.)

11
A Symphonic Composition

Oral communication is a complicated process. It involves far more than the mere utterance of sounds packaged as words. It may well be compared to a symphonic composition in music because there are four sections involved: the sounds, the intonation pattern, the stress pattern, and the body language. The native speaker has acquired all the procedures involved and so is unaware of them. But these four "sections" of communication are different in every language. Changing from one language to another may be likened to transposing from one musical key to another. Yet it is a far more complicated matter than transposing, say, from C to F.

To begin with, once the complexity of the transposition is understood, mastering it can be a fascinating problem. Fascinating, too, can be control of another language merely for the fun of it. Teachers do not seem to emphasize this point. Whatever its utilitarian value, it is an experience every educated person should have. It requires expert instruction, a real gift for mimicry, and a teacher with an ear for language.

Exactly as the string section of an orchestra may set the tone and form the essential background of a symphonic composition, so those strings of sounds, packaged as words, set the tone of an utterance. They may identify the orchestra, and they identify a speaker so that each voice is unique and can be recognized. There must be no false notes (mispronunciations) or the symphony (sentences) will be severely damaged, distracting the attention of the listener from the message.

A major scale in one key is not the same as that of another; some notes in the one are not heard in the other, and there will be new notes to include. Thus, in transposing from the "key" of English to the key of French, we no longer hear the consonants that begin the following English words (each word begins with a single consonant, sometimes spelled with more than one letter); *chin, gin, thin, then, hunt.* On the other hand, new sounds (notes) in the new key will have to be added, for example, the vowel sound in *vu*. *Vu* is not in our English major scale (sound pattern) and has to be acquired. People are prone to pronounce *déjà vu* as if *vu* were *vous*, and thus are really saying "already you." This dissonance is damaging. Likewise the "*son mouillé*" in *vieille* must be learned. Ink marks on a page cannot teach these sounds. If we pronounce the French word *très* as if it were English *tray*, we make four mistakes: The first consonant in this word is pronounced with the tongue behind the upper teeth (not the gums as in English). There is no puff of breath following (no aspiration) as there is in English. The /r/, as most people know very well, is different (uvular in French), and the final vowel sound is just that—a short vowel in French. In English *tray*, we trail off with a diphthong.

The second section of our symphony is the intonation pattern, which lends a distinctive background to an utterance. Our intonation pattern, quite unlike that of French, must be altered. We habitually end an ordinary declarative sentence with a rise on the next-to-last syllable and a drop on the last. "Pleased to meet you," and "See you tomorrow," as generally spoken in routine fashion, illustrate this. This is not the way of French.

The third section is the stress pattern. Again, our pattern is unique, entirely different from that of French. For example, we can say, and be clearly understood through our stress pattern, the difference between, "We have a French *teacher* this year, but we do not have a *French* teacher." The sounds are the same, but not the meaning. A black bird may not be a *blackbird*. One cannot do this in French. It takes hours of practice to acquire the stress pattern of another tongue (key).

The fourth section, body language, can involve elements that overwhelm the other three sections. Experts claim that most of the meaning conveyed in person-to-person oral communication comes through body motions and facial expressions. Yet the native speaker is quite unaware. Body language differs sharply from language to language, from culture to culture. The finest pronunciation may be ruined by blunders in gestures, posture, or facial expressions. A joke which is more than a joke is the statement, "Don't look at me in that tone of voice." Mastery of body language requires hours of practice and observation together with expert instruction.

A word of caution is in order here. The native speaker of, say, French, is not more likely to be aware of what is done in the intonation, stress, or body language areas than is the native speaker of English. The idea that a "native speaker" is the ideal teacher of a foreign language, long held in the highest regard, must be further examined.

The astonishing thing about our symphony of oral communication is that the speaker acts simultaneously as composer (decides what is to be said), as director (how it shall be said), and as performer (managing the detailed and simultaneous operations of each of the four "sections"). Hands will move, bodies shift, intonations vary, stress change, all at once and all according to complicated and settled cultural customs. One who masters another language must accomplish a formidable feat.

12
Stress and Intonation

In English we hear four degrees of stress and four levels of pitch as we speak (see chapter 2). We rarely think of them or study them and in general are quite unaware of their significance. Only occasionally can we adequately represent them in writing. Capital letters can signal the grammatical difference between CONtract and conTRACT, PERmit and perMIT, in which stress is the morpheme that distinguishes between noun and verb. This is a grammatical feature not found in French or Italian, for example.

Our stress morpheme allows us to produce three different meanings with the words *white* and *house*. Heavy stress on the first syllable signals the home of the President. But the pattern is different when we say, "Mine is the white house on the corner." Still different it is if we say, "Old Doc White built that house on the corner. He doesn't live there any more, but we still call it the 'White' house." See how mere ink marks on a page cannot possibly represent a language. The single quotation marks give a signal, but do not tell one what to do. In our grammar we also use pauses. A pause figures in the difference in meaning of the first two and the last two words of the following: "Long Island is a long island." Not only is the stress pattern different, there is a pause between the last two words that is not shown in our writing.

When we hear the words *strong heart* with equal stress on each syllable, we know that reference is made to an organ of the body. But if the two syllables are put together (written as Strongheart), we hear a reference perhaps to an Indian chief or a race horse. A wild cat may be Tabby on a tear if the two syllables are treated alike. But a wildcat is something else, and we signal that in writing by putting the two words into one. A HOTdog is not the same thing as a hot DOG. The former wants mustard, the latter, water.

We are now ready to correct a mistake usually made in uttering the proverb "People who live in glass houses shouldn't throw stones." The British call a "greenhouse" a *glasshouse*. The proverb refers to a place where plants are grown, not to a dwelling.

The most popular set of illustrative syllables is light, house, and keeper. With heavy stress on the first, we refer to someone aiding navigation. Stress on the second refers to a domestic duty. Another stress refers to a housekeeper who weighs only ninety pounds. Writing does not signal this; you have to hear it.

The boy home from school may ask, "What are we having for dinner, mother?" The cannibal child could ask, "What are we having for dinner? Mother?" The telltale juncture we signal with a question mark. With our change of stress, we can signal in speech.

When we put heavy stress on the word *just*, it rhymes with *must*. That is the way it is pronounced when we refer to a decision of some kind. It is also said that way when one is scolding a child, "I *just* told you to be careful." But most of the time, the usage meaning "only a while ago" has a different vowel (phonetically called "barred i"), as mentioned elsewhere, and is often pronounced "jist." In rapid speech, this vowel is often virtually discarded. Listen to people as they use it.

Stress is involved in the word *what*, generally pronounced /wat/. But again, if Dick is being scolded, mother will start this word with an /h/: "Just Hhhwat did I tell you?" Note the backward spelling of this word and *when, why, where*, and the freak *who*.

Like any other language, English has intonation melodies, especially prominent in questions. Those that end in a rising pitch are hopeful or signify interest. "Johnny, there's a chocolate bar you can have." In "Where is it?" Johnny will use a rising tone. But in "Johnny, put your shoes away at once" we hear a falling tone "Where are they?" if Johnny doesn't want to bother with his shoes. If a golfer says, "I made a hole in one yesterday," anyone who is interested in golf and the golfer may reply with a four-note melody ending with a rising pitch "You di-i-id?" But one who is merely bored may respond with a two-note falling melody "Did you?"

So we can try, in type, to represent some of this intonation. Our stylized intonation offers many patterns, including "calling contours." With a bit of difficulty we can represent some of them if we understand that type on a lower line stands for lowered pitch.

```
John          din          get
    ny come to     ner, come and     it.
```

For a three syllable name, we might hear:

```
    an      tele
Alex   der,      phone.
```

"Your tire's flat" may be spoken with the same pitch on each syllable. But if the motorist says, "What did you say?" we may hear:

```
        tire's
Your            flat.
```

A kind of contemplative contour is heard in,

```
Let's                    s
    see;                 l            e
                     i            r
                 a            i        mon
        we need  n        and  w    and     ey!
```

Calling contours come in all shapes and sizes. We acquire them naturally. They vary, they express meaning, and they form an important part of our grammar, just as stress does.

We have another interesting quirk to our stress pattern. Consider the words we use for roads, paths, highways, and routes for vehicles or pedestrians. If the name happens to be "street," we put our stress accent on its modifier, MAIN Street; otherwise the stress is on the names of the road or route: We say Fifth AV-enue, and Forty-SEC-ond Street. It is Kennedy BOULevard, Long LANE, Winding WAY, River ROAD. Yet we have a nice exception (what statement about grammar does not?): We say BRIDLE path, DEER path or DEER crossing. Do we reserve this for animal routes?

What might look like a conflict is the title of "Street Road" for a route. Our rule applies; for we say Street ROAD.

PART THREE

LEARNING FROM LANGUAGE

13
The Greeks Had a Word for It

Our vocabulary owes a great deal to Greek. From it we have not only technical terms (which have the advantage of being understood by speakers of many different languages) but many common words.

Homer described the sheep of the Cyclops as "violet-dark." This is a striking metaphor and reminds us that we do not have any reliable "color chart" to tell us exactly what a Greek or Latin word means. But Homer's word was *iodnephes*, and we have taken it in *iodine*, which is a violet-dark liquid. The Cyclops himself got his name from "circle-eye." The first element, *kuklos* in Greek, gives us *cycle, bicycle, cyclamen* (named from the bulbous roots), and *encyclopedia.* From the second, *ops*, "eye," we have *optometry, ophthalmology, autopsis* (self-eyeing), and *synopsis.*

For Homer, dawn is *rhododactylos*, "rosy-fingered." So we have *rhododendron*, "rose tree," and *dactyl*, which means "finger," the name for a certain metric foot which occurs in poetry (it has a long syllable and two short ones, like the bones in a finger). *Dendron,* "tree," gives us *dendrology* (botanical study of trees), *philodendron,* "tree love," and the first element of *Druid* (member of the tree cult).

"Wine-dark" is *oinops*, which Homer uses to describe the sea. From it we have *oenologist*, an expert in wines, and from its Latin cousin, *vinum, wine, vine, vintage,* and *vinegar*, which is sour wine.

Without Greek we would have none of the *-cracy* ("power") words: no *autocracy, democracy*, indeed, no *bureaucracy*. There would be no *-ologies*: no *biology, sociology, technology, zoology*. Nor would we have *anthems, apostles, bishops,* or *dioceses*. One could not be called a *Baptist, Catholic, Episcopalian,* or *Presbyterian*, or even a *Christian*. However, the *Devil* would be missing, too.

Without Greek we would not have the words *oyster, butter, sardines, celery,* or *asparagus*, not to mention *cherries, dates, currants,* or *absinthe*. What would life be like without *melons, marmalade, chestnuts,* or *pumpkins*? What would we call *hyacinths, crocuses, lilies, geraniums, orchids,* or *asters*? Musicians would miss the *xylophone*, and surgeons the *zyster*.

This *theme* may sound *archaic*. However, we would not be able to be *hysterical, melancholy,* or *dyspeptic*. We could hold no *dialogues*, compile no *catalogs*, see no *aerobatics* (or photograph them for that matter, for all the *-graphs* would be missing). But it would not be all bad: There would be no *rheumatism, diphtheria,* or *emetics*; and indeed no *stomachs* at all. *Asthma, anemia,* and *quinsy* would not bother us, nor would *narcotics, arsenic, toxins,* or *microbes*.

Schools would have no *scholars, desks, schedules, diplomas,* and no *pedagogues* of *arithmetic* and *geometry*; nor would we have *gymnasiums* or *athletics*. We could not have any *charity* or *eleemosynary* institutions, no *alms*, in fact; for this word is what is left of Greek *eleemosune* (pity, after all the slurring and abbreviating of centuries of travel through the mouths of people).

A fine example of the various ways in which languages treat an imported word is the Greek word for "overseer," *episcopos*. The second element has given us English *scope*; and we might turn the whole word into Anglo-Saxon *overviewer*. The German form of the word is *Bischof*; the English, *bishop*; the Danish, *biskop*; the Italian, *vescovo*; the French, *évêque*; the Spanish, *obispo*. (Note that only in Spanish and French has any trace of the first vowel sound remained.)

This *graphic sketch* hardly scratches the surface of the gifts of Greek. Others are to be found in your *lexicon*. Greek must not be *ostracized*.

14
Latin Is the Answer

Essential to the survival of our society is clear and precise communication. Communication rests chiefly on words, and clarity, on the right words. Studies have concluded that size of vocabulary has much do with the ability to think clearly and accurately.

So vocabulary must be first in any plan of education at any level. It should receive more attention than anything else. How to build up a vocabulary? It does not grow through the mere memorization of words. It is only in context that words have meaning. We can help our tennis strokes by hitting balls against a backboard, or our golf swing by hitting from a practice tee. But we must put into a game, the real thing, what we have been trying to learn in practice.

The best way to improve vocabulary and precision in choice of words is to go up against another language, especially one that differs in structure, and try to translate it into English that (a) does not sound like a translation, and (b) gets the precise meaning of the original. Latin provides an ideal medium. Its grammatical structure is quite different from that of English, and it is impossible to get the right results by translating word for word. To understand the meaning requires exact choice of words. Therefore, translation requires a good deal of thinking about which word is the best; it stretches vocabulary and makes one think hard about words. Latin, for example, has no "definite" or "indefinite" article, and a translation into English involves a consideration of how best to use these words.

Latin vocabulary itself, under proper guidance, leads to growth in vocabulary in English, especially through words that are derived from Latin. *Videre,* "to see," with past participle *visus,* "seen," provides an elementary example. To *provide* is to see ahead, and a *provision* is a looking ahead (*provisions* in the pantry look ahead to future meals). To *revise* is to look back. Teachers must show students that cognates in English are *wit, wisdom, wise*, and that the word is also seen in *vista, view*, and *visa*. Such is the sort of vocabulary tour that should occur in every Latin class every day as opportunities arise. Teachers induce students to think about words.

A good Latin book introduces mythology, perhaps the only chance a student has to get a glimpse of it. From it comes an understanding of literary allusions, leading to an enhancement of vocabulary.

Appreciation of Latin, as with other attainments, can result only from study. How can anyone understand the fine points of baseball who has never played it, watched it, and thought about it? Who can comprehend the beauty of the work of a painter or the skill of a musician? Only one who has studied painting and music. The appreciation and satisfaction that come from study are impossible to explain to those who lack such experience. A course in Latin illustrates the goal of a good school: students make mental efforts under criticism, learn to be attentive, and develop the art of expression.

15
Latin Brought to Britain

We imported thousands of words from Latin during the Renaissance, when the revival of learning took place. But the British language had absorbed many words during the Roman occupation of Britain. Claudius conquered the south of Britain in 43 A.D. Roman influence extended well to the north, too, and was notably strong in such places as York (Latin *Eboracum*), where a large military establishment was located.

One would suppose that Latin would have become a second language since it was the language of the rulers. After all, Latin supplanted the local languages in France, Spain, Portugal, and, to a lesser extent, Romania. But Latin domination did not last long enough in Britain. A number of words did become part of the British language and remained after the Anglo-Saxon conquest. Many words refer to the advanced technologies involved in the Romans' higher standard of living. For example, the Romans cooked in a *coquina*, whence our word *kitchen*, a new area for a dwelling in Britain. Romans used a *catillus*, a "pot"; hence *kettle*. They ate off a *discus*, English *dish*. A local language adopts the words for new objects and new ideas from those who bring them in.

As traders, the Romans brought in things we call *peas, plums, butter,* and *wine*. All these words come from Latin or through Latin from Greek. Traders used their own weights. The Latin word for "weight" was *pondus,* and it came to mean a specific weight; hence our word *pound*. After all, when we *ponder* something, we weigh it, and a *ponderous* speech is (over)weighty. Merchants also had to measure. *Uncia* meant "one-twelfth," and gives us *inch,* a twelfth of a foot, and *ounce,* which is one-twelfth of a pound in apothecaries' weight. A Roman innkeeper was a *caupo*. He bought supplies, and sometimes he got them cheap; hence our word *cheap*. But the meaning of "buyer" remains in the proper name *Chapman* (a buyer).

Wherever the Romans settled, they built a fort, a *castra*; and this word survives in many modern place names: *Chester, Lancaster, Worcester, Winchester*. The word for a camp or fort was taken into Arabic as *qasr,* and is seen with Arabic *al,* "the," in *Alcazar*. A Roman village was a *vicus,* and we see it in *Brunswick* (Brown's Town), and *Greenwich* (Greentown). The Romans built a *via strata,* which was a paved road; hence our word *street. Stratford* is simply "Street Ford."

English retains other ancient importations. Latin *lacus* is *lake, montem* is *mount, puteus,* which meant "a well," is *pit*. A Roman mile was a thousand paces, *mille passus*. A pace was not the distance from the mark of one foot to that of the other, but to where the same foot came down again. It was equal to about five feet, so that we can say that a Roman mile was about 5,000 feet, and so shorter than ours; and when we say "mile," we say "thousand."

16
Some Words about H

Speakers of English vary in the way they pronounce words written with initial *H-*. Thus, people have long made fun of cockney speech; Professor 'Iggins labored with Eliza Doolittle in George Bernard Shaw's *Pygmalion*.

We often hear "yoomun" for *human*, and "yoomid" for *humid*. Sometimes we hear an /h/ where it does not really belong. Nobody speaks of *an* history; yet we often hear someone refer to *an* historic occasion. Does the use of *an* for *a* seem to lend prestige to the next word? Or is it cockney speech appearing in our midst?

Thanks to the Roman poet, Catullus, who wrote in the first century B.C., we know that the Romans had trouble with this initial aspirate /h/. Indeed one of his poems could be entitled, "Get the *H* out of here." He tells us that one Arrius (we can call 'im 'Arry) was wont to begin words with /h/. He used to say, for instance, *chommoda* for *commoda* (we could render it as *hadvantage* for *advantage*). He said *hinsidias* for *insidias* (hambush for ambush). Catullus says that when 'Arry went off to the Near East, "everyone's ears had a rest until the 'orrible news came that the *Ionian* Sea was now the *Hionian*."

What made 'Arry's 'abit particularly annoying must have been the fact that initial /h/ in Latin was weakly sounded. This initial consonant simply vanished in late Latin. Thus Latin *honorem* is Italian *onore*, and we too have followed suit. For we begin our word *honor* with a vowel, not with /h/. Yet we have restored the letter *H* as French has done in *honneur*. This is simply a nod to Latin.

'Arry must have known some Greek, which did have initial aspirates in many words. So when he put one into Latin, he thought he had spoken in a learned fashion; "wonderfully well," as Catullus puts it. It was the familiar case of the untutored trying too much. We hear the same sort of sad sounds when people, fancying that they are sounding "Frenchified," say "lawn-joo-ray" for *lingerie*, missing the mark by a mile.

Catullus shows us that in Roman times people were quite as much aware of how others spoke as we are today.

17
Roots and Rudiments

Belfry is a form of the German *Bergfriede*, "place of safety," and has nothing to do with bells. Such towers, places of safety, were used as watchtowers, and so contained warning bells.

Kickshaw is from French *quelque chose*, "something," and *May Day*, the distress call, is for French *m'aider*, "to help me" (a polite infinitive, by the way, and not an imperative form). If you have been left in the *lurch*, you need not roll sideways as a drunkard, for the word has no connection. It is from French *lourche*, the name of a game. As we use it, it means a decisive defeat, as in cribbage when you double your opponent's score. Some cribbage addicts call that "skunking."

If you give up something for *the nonce*, it is etymologically for "the ones." The initial N- on *nonce* was an ending on an old form of *the*. "Then ones" turned into *the nonce*.

A *lamen* is a thin plate. So something that is *laminated* has been cut into thin plates (layers). With the difference of just one letter, we have Latin *limen*, "threshold." Anyone who is bounced from a bar must go over the threshold in order to be *eliminated*. The threshold of consciousness is just above the *subliminal*.

Change a vowel again to find Latin *lumen*, "light." We now sensibly measure the output of light bulbs and such in lumens, for wattage is not an accurate measure of the amount of light. The root *lu-* seen here gives us *lucid*; an explanation that throws light on a subject is an *elucidation*. In fact, it is *luc-sna*, which turns into Latin *luna*, "moon;" it gives light to the night. Indeed, the word *moon* comes from a root that means "measure," for the moon, to primitive people, was the most useful measurer of time; it tells the time of month.

Latin *gregem* should be found in any list of etymologies. Meaning "flock," it gives us *gregarious*, for someone who likes company, *congregate*, flock together, and *segregate*, flock apart. *Egregious* means simply out of the flock, unusual, and should not carry any special implication of disapproval. But pejoration has worked here, as it so often does; and now we may hear, "It was an *egregious* mistake." The adjective implies that the mistake was inexcusable and serious.

Latin *scintillare*, from which we have *scintillate*, means "sparkle." French reversed the C and the T and now has *étinceler*. We have dropped the E- and have *tinsel*, the sparkling stuff.

We go back to Persian for *naranj*; a *naranj* is now an *orange*. But Spanish did not make this change; the word is *naranja* in Spain.

Tattoo is Dutch for "tap to." Here, the *tap* is the "taproom" and *to* means "close," as when we say, "Shut the door to." So the *tattoo* was a signal to military folk to come back to barracks and to the bars to close up shop. *Tattoo*, a mark on the skin, has no connection. It comes from a Tahitian word.

If you are *intoxicated*, you are literally poisoned. *Toxon* in Greek is a "bow" with which you shoot poisoned arrows; it is "stuff shot from bows." So an *antitoxin* is actually "against the bow."

"That's good old Jonesey. He's always couth, gruntled, and mayed."

French *gaufre* means "honeycomb." It also means "waffle" from the honeycombed surface of this excellent food. It also gives us *gopher*, the animal that makes honeycombed burrows. *Chowder* is an Anglicizing of French *chaudière*, "cooking pot."

Sassafras comes by way of Spanish, which in turn comes from Latin *saxum*, "rock," and *fra(n)gere*, "break," because it grows through rocks. We see *frag-* "break," in *fragile* and *fragment*, and after a trip through French, as *frail*.

An extraordinary assortment of unrelated words has come to us from Arabic: *alcove*, *ghoul*, *julep*, and *tuna*.

Mew is an old word for "cage." Birds belonging to royalty were kept in a small street in London which came to be called "mews." Now the name is applied to many such small streets.

18
Shadow-Tail Squirrel, Cave-Dweller Jenny Wren

Greek *skia* (shadow) appears in its Latin cousin, *ob-scurus*, from which we get *obscure* (shadowy). Combined with Greek *oura* (tail), it gives us *skiouro* (shadow-tail), a splendid name, indeed, for squirrel. *Ailouros* (wave-tail) is the word for cat in Greek.

The *otter* is the "water-one," for it contains the same root *wed-* as in English, water and wet. The *skunk* and the *raccoon* get their names from the Algonquin Indians. Because of its shape, the *dolphin*'s name comes from the Greek for "womb," *delphos*. *Adelphos*, Greek for "brother," means "from the same womb." The City of Brotherly Love is *Phil-adelphia*.

Wolf contains a root seen in the proper names, Ralph, Adolph, and Wolfram. The Latin is *lupus* from which we have *lupine*, which may mean wolf-like, or refer to the flower, so called because it was thought to destroy the soil. The Greek cousin word is *lukos*. Combined with *anthropos* (man) it gives us *lycanthrope* (wolf-man) and *lycopodium* (the flower that means wolf's foot).

The *ferret* is the sneaky one. Its name contains the root seen in *furtive* (Latin *fur* means thief). The *weasel*'s name is from a root meaning slime, mud. *Ooze* comes from the same source. The *badger* is named for the white mask (badge) on its forehead. American Indians gave us the names for *caribou*, *chipmunk* (a regional name is ground squirrel), *moose*, *possum*, *skunk*, and *terrapin*.

Goblins join other nocturnal animals, and their name has a root *ku-*, meaning hollow place. *Kobolds*, on the other hand, are underground creatures. Their name is related to *cobalt*, an element found in the ground. We have already seen some of the cognates sharing Latin, Germanic, and Sanskrit roots. So it will not be surprising to find that the word for *mouse* in Latin is *mus*; in German, *Maus*; in Sanskrit, *mus*.

The *sloth* is a slow creature (same source as slow). A *porcupine* gets it name from Latin *porcus* (pig) and *spina* (thorn). We have cast out the /s/ in our word. The word *fox* is from a root meaning bushy-tailed, appropriately enough. It is interesting to find the female, *vixen*, with a voiced /v/ replacing the voiceless /f/.

Both *walrus* and *whale* mean big fish. The *lynx* gets its name from the root *luc-*, meaning light, thanks to its bright eyes. The root in *seal* means drag, and the *beaver* is the brown one, having the same root as *bruin*, *brown*, and *bear*.

As to bird names, the late Charles A. Choate, one of the world's great ornithologists, interested in the etymologies of bird names, pointed out that *peregrine* in peregrine falcon means "through the fields." That is where a peregrination goes. *Pilgrim* is our form of the same word. It all goes back to Latin *agrum* (field).

The *wren* belongs to the family of *troglodytidae*, in which we see the Greek *troglos* (hole, cave) and *dyein* (creep in, enter). So the *troglodyte* (cave man) and Jennie Wren creep together.

A *merganser* is a diving duck; the first element we see in English *merge*, and the second is Latin for "duck." *Loons* are *gaviidae* (Latin *gavia*, sea mew). The word contains what we call an echoic root, *la*, for the cry of the loon. This root is seen in *lament* and in *lallation*, which means making echoic sounds. Some people have a habit of echoing the last word or words uttered by a speaker. This is called echolalia.

The *petrel* belongs to the family, *hydrobatidae* (water-walkers). Greek *hydro-* is a common enough prefix, as in *hydroelectric*; the second element is in *acrobat* (high walker). A *fulmar* is named for Norse *full* (foul) and *mar* (sea). *Procellariidae* are from Latin *procella* (stormy blast). *Spoonbills* and *ibises* are *threskiornithidae*, a combination of Greek for "worship" and "bird." We see the second element in *ornithology* and in *erne* (sea eagle), a word indispensable for crossword puzzles.

Penguin is Welsh for "white head." But penguins we know do not have white heads. The name refers to a headland in the North Atlantic where they were found. The *plover*'s name is from Latin *pluvia* (rain). Why?

We cannot make head or tail of the etymology of *ducks* and *drakes*, and even the origin of the word *bird* is uncertain. But we do know that *howl* and *owl* are from the same source; the bird is logically named for its noise. A *falcon* is literally a gray bird, and the *pheasant* is named for a river in the Caucasus. *Goose* is an Old English word, related to gander and appearing in the middle of *smörgås-bord*. *Smör* means "fat," by the way.

Latin *juncus* means "reed." So a *junco* is a reed bird, and a *jonquil* is a reed flower. Hereby hangs a tale, for in other times some ropes were made out of reeds and therefore were inferior. This is the origin of our word *junk*, inferior stuff.

19
Say It with Music, Say It with Flowers

In *symphony*, a "voice-with," the voices of the instruments join with one another. In ancient Greece, the *orchestra*, from the word for "dance," was a place of performers, a semicircular space in front of the stage. Its name has been transferred to the group that performs there. The "baton" of the leader comes through French *bâton*, from the Latin *bastum* for "stick." *Bâton Rouge* in French means "Red Stick." We see this word in its Spanish form in *bastinado*, a "beating with a stick." The circumflex in the French form over the *â* is a monument to the lost Latin *s*.

Dictionaries cannot help us much with the etymology of *violin, viola, violoncello*. At least we know that it has no connection with *violet*. We get an *o* after the *l* in the violoncello. It is from Italian *violone*, which contains a suffix meaning "large." One might expect an *i*.

The English have made French *haut bois* (high wood) into *oboe*, and the *bassoon* reflects *basso*, the low-pitch woodwind. *Piccolo* is Italian for "small," and *flute* is from Latin *flare* (blow) but *flautist* contains another spelling of this root. The *flageolet*, to be sure, has the same root, which is also in *inflation*, blown-up tires and prices. Latin *clarus* (clear) is the source of *clarinet*. The word *bugle* has the same source as *bovine*, coming from Latin *buculus* (ox). It is hard to imagine how an instrument that set Tennyson's wild echoes flying could have any connection with kine.

Two of the brasses, the *sousaphone* and the *saxophone*, are named for their inventors, John Philip Sousa and A. J. Sax. The *French horn* was the *cor de chasse* of the chase.

A *trumpet* is a small trump (Shakespeare, "farewell . . . the shrill trump" in *Othello*). A *trombone* is a large one. It is originally a German word, but appears here with an Italian suffix which means "large," as in *violone*, already mentioned. In Latin a *tuba* was a straight horn. How it has changed!

As one youngster said, a percussion instrument is "anything that goes bang or tinkle." Latin *percussus* means "struck." We do not know the derivation of *chimes* or *harp*, but *piano* is short for Italian *pianoforte*, literally "soft-loud." *Cymbal* is from Greek for "cup," a concave affair, and *timpani* is an Italian plural of *timpanum* (kettle drum). The Latin *tympanum* means "drum." *Xylophone* is Greek for "wood sound," and *Glockenspiel* in German means "bell play." The *celesta* makes heavenly sounds, from Latin *caelum* to French *ciel* (sky), and the *triangle* describes itself.

An *organ* is a machine that works, such as an organ in the body. The word has the Greek root *erg-* (work) that we see in *energy*, *liturgy* (work for the people), and *surgery* (hand work). It is also the source of *orgy*. We have the root in *work* and *wright*, as in *playwright*, *wheelwright*, *cartwright*. The past participle of the verb is either worked, from work, or wrought, from wright. Thus we have an etymological choice of being either *worked up* or *wrought up*.

The names of flowers are not all from Greek; some are from Latin. We have already mentioned *lupine* (wolf-like). But *dent de lion* is French for "lion's tooth," which we have as *dandelion*. Those who know French may know the other name for this flower: *pis-en-lit*. Since the *delphinium* resembled a dolphin, it was named so; and from the same source comes *Dauphin*, the son of the King of France. His coat-of-arms bore three dolphins. *Gladiolus* is Latin for "little sword," so named from the shape of its leaves. Latin *nasus* (nose) and *tortus* (twisted) give us *nasturtium* (the nose-twister). The root of the second element is seen in *torture*, *contortion*, *torque*.

Greek *anthos* means "flower." We see it as a suffix in many names. An *anthology* is a "gathering of flowers." The *chrysanthemum* is a "gold flower," and a *helianthus* a "sunflower." A *heliotrope* turns to the sun. The *amaranth* is the "unfading flower."

Azalea contains a root meaning "dry." Azaleas can grow in dry ground. *Coreopsis* contains the root of the Greek word for "bedbug." It is the shape of the seeds that suggests the name. *Cypripedium* means the foot of the goddess Venus of Cyprus (the island where Venus was said to have been born). Our name for this flower, *lady slipper*, is appropriate, as is another name for it, *moccasin flower*.

Alyssum is Greek for "anti-rabies." It was thought to be a cure. One of the many *worts* (plants) is *mugwort*, in which the first element comes from Latin *musca* (fly). That word also gets to us by way of Spanish as *mosquito* (little fly).

Pansy is from the French for "thought," *pensée*. *Salvia* means "healing." So does *salve*; and the root is seen in *sage*, the plant. *Iris*, the multihued goddess of the rainbow, has given her name to the flower. The other name for this flower, *flag*, is from a word for "reed, rush." The *hyacinth* was supposed to have sprung from the blood of the Greek youth, Hyacinthus, who was accidentally killed by Apollo. A hyacinth when used as a gemstone may be called *jacinth*.

As flowers grow from roots, so do their names.

20
Things Are Not What They Seem

False etymologies are easy to come by. Perhaps the most common is that of *sincere*, which was supposed to come from Latin *sine* (without), as in *sinecure* (without care) and *cera* (wax), though how this derivation tallied with the meaning was not discovered. The word actually contains two elements, the first meaning something like "one, same," and the second the root in *Ceres*, goddess of the harvest and symbol of "fruit." A reasonable meaning is "all fruit, all pure." *Acorn*, which has no connection with corn, is from this same root for "fruit."

Checkmate represents two Arabic words: *shah* (king) and *mat* (dead). So when you checkmate your opponent, his king is dead.

A *dormouse* has no connection with a door. The first syllable comes from French *dormir* (sleep). So we have a "sleepmouse."

A *drawing room* is not where artists work, but a "withdrawing room."

The *wig* of *earwig* means insect, one that was supposed to penetrate the human ear. A *hamburger* has nothing to do with ham, but is short for hamburger steak from Hamburg. A *mushroom* has nothing to do with mush or room. It is French *mousseron* turned into two English words.

The *fast* of *steadfast* does not refer to either speed or not eating. It means fixed, and we have it in the expression hold fast and in fast asleep. It is also the final element in *shamefaced*, which means held in shame.

Walnut gets its first syllable from what was probably a Gaulish word. The Latin word for it was *nux Galliae*.

Welsh *rabbit*, that splendid concoction of cheese and cream, has a name that apparently did not sound sufficiently dignified. So it now turns up here and there as "rare bit."

People not only turn foreign words into words that fit their own language, but replace rare words with common ones. A most interesting example is found in French in the famous story of Cinderella. The title in French is *Le Pantoufle de Vair* (The Squirrel-Fur Slipper). The word *vair* was comparatively rare, and so when the story was read aloud, it was taken for *verre* (glass), a common word, a homonym of *vair*. Thus we have that tale all wrong. Of course, nobody could walk in glass slippers anyway; whereas a fur slipper must have been very comfortable and no doubt handcrafted.

A *woodchuck* (otherwise known as a groundhog) probably gets its name from an Indian word meaning "fisher," and so has no connection with chuck or wood.

21
Diminutives: Piglets, Goslings, and Lambkins

English has a number of suffixes that signal small size, or attractiveness, or sometimes gender. A *lambkin* is a little lamb, a *manikin*, a little man, an anatomical sketch of the body. A *napkin* is a small piece of napery, and *Jenkin* (originally without the final -s) means little John. From Dutch *vierdel* comes *firkin*, little fourth, a fourth of a barrel. *Catkin* gets its name from the resemblance of its flower cluster to a kitten's tail. In *babykins, sonnikins, kiddykins* we find a coy and affectionate meaning. No doubt, given this touch of tenderness in the suffix, we regard a *devilkin* as only a minor offender.

The suffix -*ling* makes "dear" into something nicer: *darling*. But it signals simply small size in *gosling, duckling*. There is a tone of disapproval in *hireling* and *princeling*. A *sib* is a blood relation; *sibling* applies only to brothers and sisters.

Small size is indicated by -*let*: *droplet, eaglet, eyelet, cutlet, streamlet*. It may denote something worn (small in size?): *armlet, wristlet, gauntlet* (little glove). Latin -*cule* indicates smallness: *molecule* (little mass), *animalcule* (microscopic animal); shortened to -*cle* in *particle* and *corpuscle*.

Another way of signaling affection is to use the pronoun *it* instead of some diminutive. We may say of a baby or a kitten, "Isn't *it* cute?"

The suffix -*ette* may be a diminutive, as in *cigarette, kitchenette*; or indicate the female gender, as in *usherette, suffragette*; or be an imitation, as in *leatherette*.

Two fine diminutives are *mitten* and *kitten*. The latter involves the word *kit*, which is used for the young of fur-bearing animals.

Incidentally, *kit*, collection of implements, is from a Dutch word for "jug." *Caboodle* may be a blend of this *kit* and *boodle*.

All sorts of things can happen in language, and the suffix *-kin* in *grimalkin* is an example. It goes back to *Malkin*, which may be a diminutive for *Mald*, a pet name for *Matilda*. So it was originally "gray Malkin," which we now write *grimalkin*. *Malkin* came to mean a hussy, a lewd woman. It also means an old female cat.

The suffix *-ddy* acts as a diminutive in diminishing the meaning of a word. *Shoddy* work is simply inept, and a *cruddy* object is repulsive but not extremely so. The *giddy* person is playfully silly or just plain dizzy, and a *fuddy-duddy* is a harmless old codger.

Pet-name diminutives are such as *Paddy* for "Pat," *Daddy* for "Dad." *Buddy*, like so many diminutives, is an affectionate term. A *baddy* isn't so very bad, and a *goody* is a nice person or something (not very big) to eat. *Caddy* is a diminutive of cadet (the younger son of a family), who assumes a minor role, such as carrying golf clubs. (*Caddy*, a box for tea, may come from Sanskrit.)

A nickname helps a child to get along with others, especially peers, to have an "easy" name, that is, one that is a monosyllable or ends in what we call a "Y-sound." Thus we want to hear *Jack* or *Jackie*, *Bill* or *Billy*, *Jim* or *Jimmy*. "What do you want to be called?" is a common question asked of a newcomer anywhere.

The story is told of a father who disliked nicknames and so named his four children *William*, *Wilhelm*, *Wilhemina*, and *Wilbur*. Of course, they came to be called respectively, *Bill*, *Butch*, *Dis*, and *Lefty*. If a nickname is not supplied, one will turn up, and it might not be a good one.

Nickname was originally an "eke-name," a name that ekes out another. But popular etymology makes strange words into familiar ones, and so we have "a nickname." After all, *Nick* is a name.

PART FOUR
UNRULY GRAMMAR

22
Grammar Divided into Three Parts

The term *grammar* is used to cover altogether too much territory. I subdivide it into three parts.

Grammar I (microlinguistics) is the study of the structure of a single language, a scientific statement which involves no value judgments. Such a study of the English language reveals that we have twenty-four consonants, nine short vowels, four levels of pitch, and four degrees of stress. Each of these components signals meaning. Grammar I tells how they do so. This is the grammar any ordinary child has mastered at a very early age (surely no more than six). It is all learned by ear. No amount of writing on the pages of a book can teach it. As mentioned elsewhere, that is why the native-born illiterate produces his tongue so very well; it all comes naturally.

Grammar II (macrolinguistics) deals with comparative grammar. It is useful because it draws attention to one's own structure. Hence the observation that English commonly identifies the subject of a verb as a word that precedes it. In "cat sees dog" it is word order that signals the subject. But in Latin, *felis videt canem* and *canem videt felis* mean the same thing because the final -m of *canem* marks it as the object. Moreover, the verb may be placed anywhere without affecting the signals for subject and object and the ending on *felis* marks it as the subject. Such a comparison not only emphasizes the different structures of two languages but is likely to call attention to a rule of English grammar hitherto not thought of by a native speaker.

Of great importance is the radical difference of the Grammar I of English from the Grammar I of Latin. It is in this area that grammarians of old went astray. Latin had been the *lingua franca* of the

Roman Empire, and it had acquired great prestige as the vehicle of learned writings. As a result, people thought that the grammar of Latin must be the one true grammar, and that English grammar had to be the same or made over artificially to conform to it. A good example comes under Grammar II. In Latin, two negatives signal a positive. Thus *nulli* means "none," and *non nulli* means "not none, some." Such a reversal is true of "learned" English, that is, it is *not unlikely* that most people who read this have been erroneously taught that two negatives always make a positive in English. How ridiculous this is may be discovered by considering that if a man cries out, "I didn't see nobody," he sends us precisely the same meaning as if he said, "I didn't see anybody." Anyone who stops to think realizes that this is so. Yet an untruth carefully learned is hard to eradicate, and one still finds those who continue to argue, in the face of the obvious, that the two statements mean something different.

The mistaken idea that Latin grammar had to be assumed to be the basis for English led grammarians to assign us six tenses because Latin had six. Yet the way the two languages signal tense is different. In Latin, the ending is changed. Thus *video* means, "I see," and *videbo* means, "I shall see." But in English we signal by using the function word shall with the infinitive, "I shall see." How could anyone think that these two structures are the same? If we say, "He speaks," grammarians tell us that the verb is the present tense. But how about, "He speaks next Tuesday; let's go hear him." Take the example, "He always speaks well." Surely in no way do we consider *speaks* as present tense. This verb, so used, is "aspective." That is, it records an aspect (characteristic) of someone, and is tenseless. This grammatical feature brings to mind, by way of Grammar II, those French verbs found with *être* in a past-time reference. For example, *il est mort* (he is dead), may also be translated as "he has died." So we who studied French were warned to find *être* and not *avoir*. The reason is simple: the verb is aspective. A condition is being described, not a time. Thus we say *il est monté*, for "he has gone upstairs." That is where he is; we learn something about his condition.

In English structure, we have no way of pinpointing the situation of a moment except by means of some circumlocutions. As shown, "he speaks" does not fill the bill. "At this instant he is speaking" can do so. Our structure lacks an "of the moment" "right now." But *momentarily* comes close. "The hummingbird paused momentarily." The trouble is that people use this word when they should use "in a moment." If a sign says, "Someone will wait on you momentarily," you had better get ready to transact your business in a trice or less.

A further look at Grammar I shows other dependence on word order, and a good example of Grammar II is again to compare English to French. We say, "I am always chasing rainbows," and the position of always is prescribed by our grammar. Yet French would say, "*Je poursuis toujours l'arc en ciel*," in which the adverb *toujours* (always) must follow the verb *poursuis*.

Our complicated ways of using the word *the* fill many a page in an English grammar book. Native speakers do not realize how complicated it is. For example, it functions exactly as a Latin adverb in "*The* more money he had, *the* better he served us."

Parts of speech are still being defined in school books as though they were Latin. A noun is defined as "the name of a person, place, or thing." This definition rests entirely on meaning. Other parts of speech are defined (supposedly) according to their function. One cannot define some elements of a whole in one way and others in another. As to our nouns, if someone says, "The zbich mbohs the gtoulth," our Grammar I tells us at once that zbich and gtoulth are nouns; yet we have no idea what they mean. A working definition of a noun is "a word that patterns with *the*." It is thus defined by how it functions. In Latin, nouns do not modify nouns. But they commonly do so in English: You go to the *bus* station to get the *station* bus. Anyone can cite hundreds of examples: *book plate, house wife, clothes line*, and so on.

English nouns often function as adverbs do in Latin; they modify adverbs, "The car stopped *inches* away." On the other hand, adverbs may modify nouns, "The *then* King of England, Charles II, gave William Penn a grant." *Outside* may be a noun, "The *outside* of the wall is cool." It may be an adverb, "He went *outside*," and mod-

"I always admire Chief Big Bear's terse style."

ify a noun, "the *outside* temperature." We also hear of the *now* generation.

Grammar III is often referred to simply as "grammar" in our confusing way. We can call it "metalinguistics." It is really a matter of sociology. For instance, the choice between *ain't* and *isn't* has nothing to do with the structure of English (Grammar I). The choice is purely sociological (see chapter 2). We must use the word that best serves us, remembering that everyone listens to us. A social worker must be careful to use homely words to avoid appearing to come from "out there," where people do not sympathize. No matter how ill-educated or how learned a listener, the person will react to the language we use and to technical terms. If, on a pier, one refers to throwing a *rope* over a *post* instead of a *line* over a *bollard*, one shows ignorance of the elements of shipping. Anyone who refers to "hard G" or "soft G" reveals an equally abysmal ignorance of phonetics. So it goes, whether we consider terminology or usage. One should avoid being critical of those who do not use what we consider "standard" speech.

23
Decimals and Defiance

Just as we are in the grip of grammar, so we are dictated to by our decimals. We count by tens (or fives) because of primitive counting on the hands. This is as good a way as any, but it is not the only way one can count. The Incas counted by twenties (why not use your feet?), a vigesimal system. We let decimals dictate the times of celebrations, and often count by decades.

In spite of this, we cling to the duodecimal system, with base twelve. For twelve is a convenient number; it is evenly divisible by two, three, four, six. We have sixty (5 x 12) seconds in a minute and sixty minutes in an hour, thus offering convenient intervals of time. Though a quarter of a dollar is twenty-five cents, a quarter of an hour is fifteen minutes. We are used to this inconsistency. The day has twenty-four (2 x 12) hours, and twenty-four is divisible by three, so we can have three watches of eight hours each, a reasonable length of time for someone to be on duty, as it happens.

It is convenient to have 360 degrees in a circle, for it provides another multiple of twelve. It was also convenient to fold a printer's sheet into twelve leaves (7 x 5½ inches), and so we call that book size *duodecimo* from Latin for "twelve." A *quire* used to consist of twenty-four (2 x 12) sheets, but now has yielded to the decimal system and contains twenty-five. But a *gross* is still 144 (12 x 12). Latin *uncia* gives us inch, a twelfth of a foot, and ounce, a twelfth of a pound, troy weight. This pound contains twenty times twelve pennyweight, or 240. We buy many articles by the twelves or dozens.

When is a decimal not a decimal? It is when we record the number of innings a baseball pitcher has pitched. Then the figure after the "decimal" point represents a third, because there are three outs in an inning. If a pitcher is taken out with one out in the fifth inning, his record will show that he pitched 4.1 innings, that is, 4⅓. (Perhaps we should call the dot in this notation a "tertial" point.)

We cling to counting by the week, a tradition that cannot be set aside. The word week, by the way, literally means "turning, change," and it is cognate with Latin *vice* as in vice-president. We have maintained a custom of the Druids, who counted by nights, not by days: To them we owe *fortnight*. We find *se'nnight* in Shakespeare's *As You Like It* and *Othello*, and *sevennight* in *Much Ado about Nothing*, additional evidence of this custom. French for "fortnight" is *quinzaine* (a fifteen) because both ends of the series of days are included. Thus, the period from 1 January to 15 January involves fifteen days, though the period covered is only fourteen.

We defy our decimals in another way when we count by the score, using the vigesimal system. There is no doubt that Lincoln's use of the word in his Gettysburg Address provided a rhetorical and appealing touch. "Four score and seven" is far more impressive than plain "eighty-seven."

The French use "four score" for eighty: *quatre-vingts*, "four twenties." *Score* is from Old Norse and originally meant "notch." A notch is a mark or a cut. When the Bad Man of the Wild West killed an opponent, he notched his trusty gun and so he literally "kept score."

Score is found in *plowshare*, the part of the plow that "cuts" the furrow, plus the word we have in *shear*, and in *shard* (a cut-off piece of pottery). It is also in both *skirt* and *shirt*, garments cut off at the bottom. It is also the source of the word *short*. With this in mind, let us keep it short and say *soon*, not *shortly*.

24
All about A

Grammarians of old (and of today) called *A* "the indefinite article," a silly name, indeed. They gave no hint that in English grammar this word, in one of its many uses, signals that a noun follows (just as *the* does).

The letter *A* is a busy one, as in the sentence, "Fat father's called away," in which it represents five different vowel sounds. All by itself it spells many words. Now we are all used to one-letter words such as *O* (the exclamation) and *I* (the pronoun), but it is unlikely that we were ever shown that we have a good many other one-letter words, each one spelled with *A* alone.

It is a cardinal number in "Not *a* man survived." It is, by origin, a collapsed form of *one*. It means "kind of" in "Birds of *a* feather flock together," or "*A* man who can do that is gifted." It describes a shape in "It is an *A*-frame house." It serves as a preposition in "two dollars *a* dozen."

It is a scholastic grade in "He got an *A* in Latin," and an abbreviation in "He won his *A* at Amherst." It is the name of a piece of type in "An *A* has fallen out of this word in this line of type." It is an algebraic symbol, and the name of a musical note: "Sound your *A*." It is also the name of that note when written on a musical score. It is an ordinal number (first) in Section *A*, Part *A*. So here we see eleven words, each represented in our orthography by the letter *A*, serving, according to Latin grammar definitions, as noun, adjective, and preposition. We have one more, the archaic "The frog who would *a*-wooing go."

From the French we have taken it in to mean "in the manner of": chicken *à* la King, pie *à* la mode. From the Latin we find it signaling the feminine gender in *alumna* (versus alumnus). It is the plural ending of certain Latin nouns, memorandum/*memoranda*. *Agenda* and *data* are really plurals, too; but they are commonly treated as singular. Another common example is *memorabilia*.

The versatile letter *A* stands for certain prefixes with various meanings. It indicates position: *afloat, ashore, astride*; condition: *aloof, aware, awake, alive, amazed*; manner: *aloud, amain* (in haste).

A and its partner *an* represent the Greek negative prefix: *atheistic, amoral, analgesic, amnesty* (here the /n/ has been turned into /m/). *A* means "again" in *anew*, and in *nowadays* it stands for "on." The word was originally an adverbial genitive "now + on + days."

Idiomatic uses are numerous and complicated. "Little did he care" (he cared little), but "He cared *a* little" (more positive). See the odd position of *a, an* in "How happy *a* party it was," "It was too awful *an* experience for him." See the solemnity of repeating *a* in "He is *a* sadder and *a* wiser man." Much more forceful than "He is sadder and wiser."

25
Hail to The

Perhaps one can still find what we used to call "Japanese flowers," small compact pieces of paper. When immersed in water, they would blossom into all sorts of shapes and beautiful colors. Perhaps the little word *the* is not so beautiful when it is immersed in the linguistic pool, but it puts on an astonishing display of meanings and uses, far beyond the imaginings of a native speaker of English, who never gives it a thought.

The is a weakened form of *that*. We find it in a still weaker form in "I saw ol' Bill, just *t'*other day." On the other hand, it can be forceful and emphatic: "Bill's just *the* man for that job."

We do not pronounce this word the same way in every context. "He crossed *the* /ə/ river and came to *the* /ij/ other side." Latin and Russian do not have any such word, but get on well enough without it. In our grammar, we would be hard put to make up for its absence.

Consider some of the oddities. We say "at night" but "in *the* evening." "He speaks French" but "The translation is from *the* French." "What is *the* French for 'mouse'?" As for diseases, sometimes we do one thing and at other times, another: "He has measles, but never had *the* mumps." We use *the* only once if parallel words are involved: "*the* Duke and Duchess of Kent."

Here is another peculiarity: we use *the* with geographical expressions that are either plural or modified. "He has been to Georgia, but not to *the* Carolinas; to Canada, but not to *the* West Indies. He crossed *the* Mississippi River and went on to *the* Atlantic Ocean." A peculiarity in French grammar is that we find en Suisse (in Switzerland) but au Canada (the preposition *à* combines with the article *le* to become *au*).

We are prone, now and then, to imitate other languages, and so, in imitation of the French, we refer to *the* Tyrol and *the* Sudan, using *the* with singular, unmodified nouns. When we say *the* Congo, we may conform to our own grammar and think of it as *the* Congo River.

This little word often conveys an important difference in meaning. "He is going to *the* prison" means something quite different from "He is going to prison." "He goes to church" does not mean the same as "He goes to *the* church." We play golf or tennis, but play *the* piano, *the* clarinet. Yet when referring to someone who plays in a band, we will say, "He plays clarinet in that combo," not using *the*. In a stage performance you may play *the* clown, just as you may play *the* lead, but if they say of you that at every party you play *the* clown, there is quite a different message.

We find this word acting the way we were told Latin adverbs act, modifying an adjective: "*The* more money he had, *the* higher his taxes." It appears as an adverb in "*the* better to serve his country."

Note the distinction between "He got there on Sunday," and "He got there on *the* Sunday; by *the* Monday, the matter was settled." (British usage, by the way, inserts *the* in both instances.) "Father is head of the household," we may say. But if we are describing some cultural pattern, we say "*The* father is the head of the household." This versatile word may mean "kind of." "*The* man who says that is an idiot." Or it may serve as a preposition "five dollars *the* pair."

"We saw Jones. He is one of *the* Joneses of Boston." In the plural a proper name is not, in strictest sense, a proper name; so it requires *the*. We commonly distinguish between singular and plural by using *the*: "We noted Walter's arrival. We noted *the* Walters' arrival." Our orthography signals the difference; but in speech we depend upon the presence or absence of *the*.

The is often omitted in a style that is supposed to be technical. As one manual of direction said, "Turn knob at left to activate radio." (Writers of this sort of stuff could not simply say "to turn on the radio.") It went on, "Turn knob at right for minimum of hiss."

This is phony and has an official air about it, as does, "Insert key, open door, push button."

What a difference there is between "He's quite an actor, isn't he?" and "He's quite *the* actor, isn't he?" Or consider, "He's not *the* Joe Smith of last year." We customarily put *the* before certain titles: "*the* Honorable Judge Smith," or "*the* Reverend Robert Jones."

What a tremendous variety of grammatical uses we find when we look at the little word afloat in the pool of English structure. Lucky are we to have acquired these features of our grammar as native speakers. What problems confront the newcomer to English! In "grammar" school did Miss Fidditch point out this complex collection of uses or simply dismiss *the* as a "definite article"?

26
Comparisons Are Often Remarkable

English oddities are found in the comparison of adjectives, especially when words taken from Latin are involved. Thus Latin supplies *juvenile/senile* and *junior/senior*, but does not offer a superlative to either. So we fall back on *youngest/oldest*. We also have *elder/eldest* to go with old. But these words are used to refer only to the comparative age of a person. Thus a person's *elder* child may be only six years old and the *oldest* only eight. It is unusual to make a noun from the comparative of an adjective, but we do that in *elder* as in "he was an *elder* of his church."

Latin had adjectives that existed only in the comparative and superlative degrees, whose positive is found only as an adverb (or preposition). Thus *ultra* (beyond) provides *ulterior* and *ultimate* (the most beyond). *Inter* and *intra* provide us with *intermission* and *intramural, interior* and *intimate* (the most inside). *Super* and *supra* have *superior* and a double superlative, *supreme* and *summit*. *Post* appears in *posterior*. The Latin superlative is *postumus* (no *h*). But Latin *humus* means "ground," and so we misspell the word in English because we think of a *posthumous* child as born after the father is "in the ground." *Ante*, the opposite of *post*, gives us only the comparative *anterior*.

Is *prime* ever thought of as a superlative? From *pro*, *prae* (before) we get *prior* as comparative, and *primus* (whence prime) as superlative. A *primer* is a first reader, and *prime* time is of first value and *prime* ribs are the best. *First*, to be sure, is itself a superlative, as are *last* and *next*. *Next* is the superlative of *nigh*. Your *nigh-gebur* (dweller) is your neighbor. The comparative is *near*; but this word has lost comparative force, and so we have made up a new comparative, using the regular suffix *-er*: *nearer*.

When we use *more* to form comparatives in longer words, we may also use *the* (as mentioned in the preceding chapter) exactly as a Latin adverb would be used: "The more money he had, the better he served his community."

As to *most* for the superlative, note that we use it sometimes as a suffix: *utmost, uttermost, outermost, innermost, uppermost, topmost, easternmost*. It has the ring of the usual suffix, *-est*.

Whereas the comparative *more*, has an /r/ sound, and therefore sounds like an ordinary comparative, *worse* and *less* do not. So *worser* occurs frequently in Shakespeare, yet is not acceptable today in Standard English. However, *lesser*, also a double comparative, is in good use, generally to compare size or importance: the *Lesser* Antilles, the *lesser* evil. *Less* is unique in being the only comparative in English that does not have an /r/ sound.

Late has two superlatives, *latest* and *last*, and they sometimes do not mean the same thing at all. The *latest* fashion (fortunately) is not the *last*. It also has two comparatives, *later* and *latter*. *Latter* goes with former, and is limited in use to such expressions as "the *latter* years of the century" or "*Latter*-Day Saints."

Though we are fond of the suffix *-est*, and like our superlatives to involve it somehow (*worst, least, most*), we accept some that do not (*prime* is an example). But we have taken some superlatives direct from Latin without change: *optimum* (all too often used for best), *maximum, minimum.* With characteristic refusal to be "regular" we never accept *pessimum* (worst).

We signal a comparative sometimes by using *too.* "He came *too* late," that is, later than was required. "This is all *too* much," that is, more than I can bear. But *too* loses most of its force in "I'm only *too* happy to oblige," just as does *most* in "I'm *most* happy to see you."

An interesting oddity is heard in words that signal their comparatives, not by adding just the ordinary suffix *-er*, but by prefixing that suffix with a /g/. "*Linger longer*, you'll be *stronger* and feel *younger.*" These noises are the same as those heard in *anger, finger.*

We say larger *than*, older *than.* But with Latin comparatives such as *prior, inferior, superior*, we use *to*; but not with *major* and *minor.* We do use senior *to* and junior *to*, though rarely.

There is a big difference between saying "She is an *older* woman," and "She is *elderly.*" *Elder* is *older* with a touch of class and deference. An *elderly* gentleman must be a much-respected member of the community. We do not respect our *olders*, but our *elders*, or an *alder*-man. The *elder* statesman is distinguished for his years of service. We are not supposed to say "old folks." Call them by Latin names: *senior citizens.* We get a still different shade of meaning in *oldsters* (Dickens used the word), a coy counterpart of *youngsters.*

Old itself often has a special meaning. "He worked for the *old Herald Tribune.*" It means "no longer in existence but lasting long enough to be still well known." It also adds a touch of nostalgia.

Ancient offers another nuance. The *Ancient* Mariner might have been even less happy if he had been called the "*Old* Sailor," as Samuel Butler pointed out. But Coleridge wanted us to see him with obligatory gray beard, optional glittering eye, a picture of an ol' feller who knowed what 'twas all about.

Erstwhile paints a different picture, often of someone who has had a significant change in status or occupation. The *erstwhile* boss may now be merely an employee. Nostalgia is also associated with *yore* (perhaps from *year*) as in "days of *yore.*" *Yesteryear*, like *yore*, has an archaic touch and is found in special contexts. It gives a graceful effect. In the eighteenth century, Thomas Percy went this one better when he wrote in *Sir Patrick Spence*, "Late, late, *yestreen* I saw the new moone/Wi' the auld moone in hir arme."

Latin *senior* means "older," and from its root we have *senate* (group of elders) and *senescence*, a word that implies getting older for the worse. *Senior* in Spanish is *señor*; in Italian, *signore*; in French, *seigneur* (a titled nobleman). But the French word is shortened to *sieur* and appears in *monsieur*. English has shortened it to *sire* and to *sir*. Unfortunately, *surly* is from the same source; are old men always surly? Well, sometimes they are *senile*. The fine Irish name *Sean*, by the way, is from this source.

27
Identical but Contrary

An example of homographs (homonym opposites) is found in the two English words spelled *plight*. The one that occurs in "*plight* one's troth" is from a Germanic root and is akin to the word *peril* (some would cynically say there is a connection here!). Another word from the same root is *pledge*. The second *plight*, (predicament, trouble) comes from a root meaning fold and is seen in Latin derivatives such as *pliant* (easily folded), *supple, two-ply, complex, implicate* (to fold into). Interestingly, *flax* is from this root, a foldable substance that can be made into a fiber.

Another pair is found in the two words spelled *gate*. One of them is simply a device to regulate the flow of something, or that permits a flow, as a *gate* in the wall. This is the *gate* in *Watergate*, which means *floodgate*. The French for this *gate*, by the way, is *écluse*.

The other *gate* means simply street and comes from an old Norse word. Our word *gait* is from the same root. So *Harrowgate*,

Bishopsgate, Notting Hill Gate in London are just Harrow Street, Bishop's Street, and so on. Naturally enough, the original meaning of this word was lost, and so we find *Aldersgate Street* in London, which means Alders-street Street. *Gate* meaning receipts is simply money taken at the gate (entrance).

Only the context can reveal the meaning of *cleave*. "*Cleave* to that which is good" (Romans 12:9). The word, from the same root as *clod*, *clot*, and *clump*, means, in the context, hold on to. The other *cleave* (cut apart) has the root seen in *cleft*, *cloven*, and, surprisingly, *glyph*. A *hieroglyph* is a sacred carving. *Clip* (cut off) and *clip* (attach) are from different roots. The latter is associated with *clamp*, *clasp*, and *clutch*.

Sometimes the very same word acquires opposite meanings. A broken leg is certainly a *handicap*; but if you have a big *handicap* in golf, you may win the prize in a net-score contest.

To *let* someone do something is to give permission. But *let* in tennis refers to a ball that hits the net, bounces into the right place, and refers to interference, not permission. So does the expression "without *let* or hindrance." Hamlet says, "Unhand me, gentlemen. By heaven, I'll make a ghost of him that *lets* me."

When a nation is subject to *sanctions*, it is interfered with. But to *sanction* an act is to approve it. To the lawyer, a case that is *moot* is done with. To the layman, a *moot* question is one still up for argument and discussion.

Latin *hostilis* meant "stranger, foreigner." Thus it came to mean "enemy," for the stranger may be *hostile*. But your *host* and *hostess* are not hostile; they are showing hospitality.

A strange reversal, which involves a series of changes of meaning, is found in *nice*, from Latin *nescius* (foolish, knowing nothing), and Chaucer uses it so. Then it came to mean "particular about trivial things," and then "particular about details." Hence a *nice* distinction is anything but foolish. Another development stems from the thought that a foolish fellow is a harmless fellow and perhaps a pleasant (*nice*) fellow to have around.

28
Word Order

So important is word order in our language, we send a special signal when we put an adjective after its noun. Thus *Lady Bountiful* from time immemorial has been portrayed as gracious, perhaps entertaining *Prince Charming*, the *heir apparent*, in her *house beautiful*, and perhaps protecting him from some *devil incarnate*. So it has been from ages past, when the *retort courteous* was the goal of the gifted. One feature of our grammar, already mentioned, is the identification of the subject of a sentence by its position before the verb, "cat sees dog."

Since French puts most adjectives after their nouns, some phrases adopted from the French retain that feature: *attorney general*, *notary public*, for example; and the plural is placed on the noun, not the adjective: *notaries public*.

French *thé dansant* meant a tea party at which there was dancing. Confused by the French word order, we have changed the adjective to a noun and vice versa, and a *tea dance* is now a kind of dance, not a kind of tea.

With the French adjective *ancien*, word order changes the meaning. When it precedes its noun, as in *ancien régime* (former regime) it means once existing, but existing no more. When it follows its noun, it means simply "old."

English is fussy about word order. It would be difficult to rearrange the words in "the little, old, fat, German doctor" and sound like English. We put the adjective of nationality before the noun: a German doctor. But French and Italian put it after, *un médecin allemand*, *un medico tedesco*, copying the Latin of which they are later versions. See the difference between "Naturally, he helped me" and "He acted naturally." We often reverse subject and verb, especially if the subject is a pronoun. "Hooray!" cried he. Or, "Wait!" shouted our guide. The reversal gives dramatic effect. "How old is he?" is something quite different from "How old he is." "You must go to bed, and so must I." Here the word *so* leads to a reversal. Reversal gives special effect, also, in such as "Money he has, but brains, no."

The so-called cardinal numbers, *one*, *two*, *three*, and so on, become ordinals when they follow a noun. Thus we locate the famous quotation "Men have lost their reason" by writing: "*Julius Caesar,* act 3, scene 2, line 110," that is to say, third act, second scene, one-hundred-and-tenth line.

Possibly the most commonly misplaced word is *only*. Yet its position makes a great deal of difference in meaning. It must stand directly before the word it modifies. "I'd buy that *only* if I had two dollars" (otherwise, no sale). "If I had *only* two dollars" (something costs more than that). "If *only* I had two dollars!" (wistful). "I owe Joe *only* two dollars" (not a big debt). "I owe *only* Joe two dollars" (all others have been paid off).

It should not be too difficult for careful writers and speakers to get this word order all right. If they *only* would!

29
Pronoun Peculiarities

A youngster is trotted out to be displayed to a gathering of adults. Upon coming to a halt, he might well say, "My how I've grown! Now may I go?"

But then there may be an Uncle Plethora, who, with false enthusiasm and genuine condescension, may say, "Ah, Little Man, and how are *we* today?" The worst of these pompous creatures are those who place a patronizing hand on Little Man's head, as though it were a newel post.

Little Man can reply, not with the humble mumble that is expected, "Very well, thank you, Uncle Plethora. I am grateful to you for getting me extra credit in English."

"How is that?" asks Uncle Plethora, taken aback (where he ought to have been taken long ago and left).

"Our teacher has been discussing odd usages in English, among them the use of the pronoun *we*. It is not uncommon, as a first-person singular, to be used by what is left of royalty, or by editors and columnists. But its use as you have used it, as second-person singular, is rare indeed outside the sick room. Nurse may say, '*We* must drink our soup to get our strength back.' That sort of usage is common enough. But I will get double credit when I quote you."

We might add to the youngster's linguistic analysis that Uncle Plethora has used one of those "nothing" words by saying "*and* how are we today?" There is nothing for *and* to connect.

Uncle P. is trying to socialize. He feels he has to say something other than a simple greeting, for in our adult culture we use language to socialize; we chatter. Other animal situations have other patterns. Monkeys groom each other as their way of socializing. Kittens romp. Dogs rush about. We chatter. The more decibels at a party, the more successful it is. "You could hardly hear yourself think," we say.

To return to Uncle Plethora (admittedly with reluctance), we note that he thinks he must get into the adult chatter pattern with a youngster, that is, "make conversation." Aunt Rotunda may try to do so, too, by asking Little Man how old he is, what grade he's in, does he like sports, and so on. The questions are usually phony, and the replies little heeded. The young one is not interested in engaging in a conversation, especially if it is silly. A courteous greeting suffices, unless the adult has something special in common with the young one, something interesting to discuss. Condescension ought not to be a use of language.

Our pronouns have additional oddities. (A pronoun is a word

that represents a noun.) In Latin, *ego* (I) came first in a string of personal pronouns. *Tu* (thou) came second, and *ille* (he) came last. As a result, we arrange the conjugation of our verbs in that order: "I am, you are, he is." But that is not at all the order of English pronouns; for *I* is always last in a string, whereas *he* is first, not third. We say, "You and I saw it. He and I saw it. He, you, and I saw it."

We do not seem to object to the inclusion of *it* among the personal pronouns even though *it* does not refer to persons. Consider the pronoun *it*, and the uses we make of it: "How far is *it* to town? I make *it* a point to wait. *It* is Sunday. *It* is raining. He has *it* made," and so on. Much in favor with those who wish to avoid attributing anything to anybody is "*It* is said that." Then there is the preparatory *it*: "*It* is clear that you cannot impose the grammar of one language on another and expect to make sense."

A fine example of the imposition is the fuss over "It's *me*." The objection to *me* rests on the fact that Latin would require *I*. But that has nothing at all to do with English grammar. The objection today rests solely upon sociology. Many people do not like the expression "It's *me*," because of what they were taught. Speakers simply must select their pronouns according to what they think will be best for them personally.

The vague *it* brings us to a few words that we call "generic" or "impersonal" pronouns, which provide the same sort of vagueness: "*One* finds that statement hard to believe." In this use, *one* is impersonal. Used as a personal pronoun is "*One* ran away, *one* stayed behind." We use *you* as a generic, and we pronounce it "*ya, yuh*." "*Yuh* can fight City Hall, if *ya* try." This is quite different from "*You*, Mr. Jones, can fight City Hall."

We have many personal pronouns: *each, nobody, somebody, all*, for instance. Sometimes we can make one of them a noun, as in "The team consists of a bunch of *nobodies*."

Demonstrative pronouns, *this, that, these, those* may turn up in plural as personal pronouns: "*These* are my friends; *those*, my enemies." We insist on word order and control when we use demonstrative pronouns. We can say, "This book *here*, that book *there*," never batting an eye or giving a thought to the fact that *here* and *there* modify book. But we were taught to object to putting those modifiers before the nouns they modify: "This *here* book, that *there* book." The French, on the other hand, have no objection, using *celui-ci* (this here) and *celui-là* (that there).

PART FIVE

MEANING, MESSAGE, AND METAPHOR

30
The Notions of the Motions

> Fenstermacher strode into the room, head thrust forward, lips drawn
> back, arms swinging at his sides, every line in his body taut. Vitrine
> Cuverte stood her ground, feet planted firmly apart. Hands on hips,
> blue eyes flashing defiance, she tossed her head in disdain.

A great deal of communicating has been going on here, and not a
word spoken. Body language plays an important role in person-to-
person communication.

Head motions are fascinating to watch, especially in a TV news
program. One anchor person made fifty-one head motions during
the time on screen in a thirty-minute broadcast. Rapid nodding signals herald vigorous agreement. A forward thrust seeks to emphasize a point. We also give other signals with the head. We can nod
a greeting to one who passes by, or we can bow the head in respect
or for emphasis. We often point with the head to indicate where
something is situated, or to recognize someone who wants to
speak. The head is bowed in reverence, or as a signal of humility or
shame.

Facial expressions differ from culture to culture. We have our
own wide variety but must remember that they may not send the
same signals in France as they do in the United States. Teachers of
other languages do not always deal with this aspect. Gestures, too,
are different. We gesticulate as much as anybody but generally with
the arms close to the sides. When others hold their arms away from
the body, they seem to us to be gesturing more forcefully. Even
within the United States, there are significant differences. One
smiles more readily in some areas than in others.

But we all, in our culture, pay great attention to the way people walk. Clear proof is the number of words we use to describe walking. At a meeting, people may stride in, lounge in, bustle in, creep, slink, stalk, storm, swagger, or slouch. The body signals are clear.

Fat folk waddle, tots toddle, the aged dodder or poke along. Young ones frisk, commuters dash or tear along, hunters prowl or stalk. The stylish damsel may mince along; others strut. When out for the air, we may amble, ramble, lope, jog, trot, swing along, loaf along, or sprint. Anyone can add many more to this list. French *allure* means "way of walking."

We take particular notice of the inebriated as our vocabulary shows: stagger, lurch, weave, sway, reel, totter. It would take a full page to list all the words we have for drunks: fried, stewed, and so on, including the old-fashioned and delicate *half-seas over* and the splendid Victorian *disguised*.

Do not tug at an ear lobe or stroke a chin or stick out a thumb in other cultures without a lesson in what these things may mean. In some places it is customary to put your elbows on a dinner table.

Ordinary hand signals guide a plane to a terminal location, inform a crane operator, ask for a ride, point to an object. For a lesson in confusing hand signals, watch the third-base coach when a runner is on first base!

But unconscious hand signals tell a tale every time. With palms together they ask for help; with cupped palms held up they may ask for money. Those are conscious positions. But simply watch a speaker. How frequent are the motions? How extensive? Speakers are usually quite unaware of how they supplement their speech with their hands. Too much motion distracts from what is being said. Is it true that women give hand signals with the wrists loose more than men do? Gestures are interesting to watch as expressions of language.

Of particular interest here is American sign language, a whole language in itself, not a way of "speaking" English or any language at all. A first-rate book is *The Signs of Language* by Edward Klima and Ursula Bellugi. A child learns sign language as a native speaker. Perhaps it is a reasonable way to a universal language.

When an audience applauds, it sends various signals of appreciation (or lack of it). Are the hands cupped? Are the arms raised at all? Are hands clapped together or do the fingers of one hand hit the palm of the other? Is there any delicate finger-tapping? A look at a typical TV audience shows a wide variety of signals and is amusing.

Common nonverbal symbols are the inverted coffee cup at a restaurant, the raised hood of an abandoned car, the white rag tied to the door handle of a stalled car, the flag flown at half mast or half staff or upside down.

An interesting study of nonverbal symbols can be made by giving each member of a group of about a dozen people a knife and a fork and asking them to place these utensils on the dinner plate as they are accustomed to do when they have finished a meal. Consider the dinner plate as the face of a clock and see "what time it is." For some, knife and fork will show about 4:20; for others, 4:40, for still others, 2:45. Some put knife and fork across the top of the plate, making chords of a circle. Important here is the lesson that no special way can be regarded as "correct," and all others "wrong." One follows the culture of the locality.

Required reading for anyone interested in body language and nonverbal symbols is *The Silent Language* by Edward T. Hall.

31
Whistling for It

When becalmed, sailors used to whistle for the wind, often with no success; hence the expression "whistle for it," which implies there is little chance of getting it.

Many parts of the world have highly complex examples of "whistle speech," by which people communicate over long distances with remarkably well-developed intonations which imitate those of the spoken language. Many years ago, an observer reported the whistle speech of La Gomera, one of the Canary Islands, and recorded its uses, its extent, and its complexity (R. G. Busnel II and A. Classe, *Whistled Languages*). Whistled speech developed, naturally enough, in a mountainous area of Turkey, where travel is difficult; it is not an isolated phenomenon.

Whistling may be done with the lips only. If you try, you can whistle "how are you?" simply by reproducing the tone pattern. A primitive example is heard in our traditional "wolf whistle" aimed at a passing female. It clearly conveys a message. We can signal astonishment in a common whistle, quite crudely represented with letters thus: *wheek-we-yoo*. If there is any proof needed that a language can be analyzed only by studying its sounds, and not by letters, this is it. We all know what the sound is, but it can scarcely be reduced to writing.

Whistle speech can be produced with one finger in the mouth, or with two. In our culture we commonly employ whistle speech as a signal for attention.

32
Tut, Tut, Tsk, Tsk, Tch, Tch

The noises that we represent by *tut, tut,* and *tsk, tsk,* and *tch, tch* are technically called "clicks." They are dental clicks because the teeth are involved in their formation. All of them are real words, for they have meanings we understand. The admonitory *tut, tut* is formed by placing the tongue behind the upper teeth and drawing it back and down. The letters we use to "spell" it give a fair picture of the noise.

But *tsk, tsk* fails miserably. We place the tongue behind the upper teeth and draw it back and upward, producing the clicking sound by drawing in the breath and pulling the tongue away from the teeth and gums. It is used to mean "too bad" in such situations as the dropping of something on the floor. This click occurs in much different form when it is used to scold a child. The child has been repeatedly warned not to rush about in a room, but does so anyway and knocks over a lamp. Then he can be admonished by a *tsk, tsk* which is uttered slowly with the lips rounded and often with shoulders raised. It clearly means "How often have I told you?" We do not "talk down" to the child; we "click down."

We have an alarmed or cautionary click in *tch, tch*. The breath is expelled while the lips are rounded, and the tongue is placed behind the closed teeth. It says to a child, "Oh you mustn't do that!" In any use, it signals concern in a rather mild way. But we have other clicks, too.

The lateral click is made by placing the tongue against the hard palate and drawing it back while the lips are pulled back. We use it to start a horse. But it has a much different use, one that I call "the click of secondary greeting." You have spoken to X with the usual greetings at the beginning of the day. When you meet up with X again, you are not likely to go through all this once more. You may very well send out that lateral click which means "I acknowledge seeing you in an informal way. We cannot be expected to say hello once again."

We have a lingual signal formed by bringing the tongue from the roof of the mouth in a "flap" forward. It may be a signal of wistfulness. "My, I wish I had a dress like that" could be followed by this tongue flap. It may also signal sympathy. Mrs. X tells Mrs. Y that Mrs. Z is back in the hospital again. To this, Mrs. Y may respond with a tongue flap that clearly means "Too bad. I'm sorry."

Our clicks are simple and naive and not used for extended communication. But the Zulus and the Xhosas, for example, are highly skilled in communicating by clicks of various kinds and put

"Never end a sentence with a Bong."

them together at some length. So from that standpoint, English is a "primitive" sort of language.

Complex messages can be sent with remarkable speed on jungle drums (John F. Carrington, *Talking Drums of Africa*). Smoke signals are also well known and provide quick communication.

The beautiful songs of birds are territorial signals, as is the hammering of a woodpecker. Dolphins whistle, as has long been known.

As we take note of the sounds sent out by other species to convey nonverbal meaning, we seldom listen to the strange noises we ourselves make. Sometimes people dismiss with disdain what they call the "grunts" and "monosyllables" they fancy they hear in other languages. But a stranger from a strange land would certainly take note of our monosyllabic grunts.

Here are some of them: uh-oh, wow, zap, tut tut, ow, hi, ho, ha, ugh, nah, huh?, ouch, eek, pshaw, phew, ooh, um-hum, ah-ha, nope, yep, yeuch.

We could offer more. Suffice it to say that native speakers are happy with the language they learned when young and are not at all concerned with the odd sounds it contains.

33
Discrimination against Women

In all the talk about discrimination against women, little or nothing has ever been said about language abuse. Never mind the trifling objections to *chairman*; "chairperson" is little more than a cosmetic change. In almost every culture on earth, women have been "talked down" by the use of derogatory terms. Racial slurs are minor compared to the slurs against women.

When the male and the female are paired in a vocabulary, the female is likely to be demeaned. Thus a *foxy* fellow is pretty smart; but a *vixen* is a "shrewish, ill-tempered woman," as the dictionary tells us. Here one word defined by another bears the same sour meaning: a *shrew*, we might say, is a "vixenish, ill-tempered woman." A *master* is in control, whereas *mistress* tells a different tale. The Indian *brave* is a stout fellow; when we call a woman a *squaw*, we insult her. There are still a few *kingdoms* around; who ever heard of a *queendom*? Even when a woman is at the head, it is still a *kingdom*. A big, strong man can be described as a *bull*. Do you call a woman a *cow*? *Sir* is a term of respect; *madam*, as we use it, may be far from that.

Few of the long string of demeaning words describe men. A *harridan* is probably a worn-out horse. It is not only witches whom we sometimes describe as *hags*. A *termagant* used to refer to a boisterous, brawling person of either sex, but is now used only of women. Deterioration of meaning is also true of *virago*, which used to mean simply a tall, strong woman. Now she is obstreperous.

Crone should get the prize, because it comes from the same root as *carrion* and *caries*. Call on a *wizard* for help, for his name contains the same root as *wise*. But the *witch*, his female counterpart, is sometimes defined as a woman "who has dealings with the devil." Add to this grisly list *slut, sloven*, and the more recent *bag* to the evidence of linguistic insult.

One of the ablest of Amazons in the fight against this sort of thing is Alleen Pace Nilsen. She has given us what she calls the "chicken metaphor" about a girl's life. "In her youth she is a *chick*, then she marries and begins feeling *cooped up*, so she goes to *hen parties* where she *cackles* with her friends. Then she has her *brood* and begins to *henpeck* her husband. Finally she turns into *an old biddy*." (Clark, Eschholz, Rosa, eds., *Language*, 207).

One enthusiastic and exasperated female friend of females everywhere has declared, with an optimism that is refreshing, "We are moving from androcentric values and behaviors to androgynous, or better yet, gynandrous, societal values. Occupations must be desexigrated." If words work magic, magic must come from this majestic declaration.

In German, the word for "girl," das *Mädchen*, is neuter. Grammatically, the word is a diminutive, and in German, as in Greek, diminutives are neuter. But "wife," *das Weib*, is also neuter.

Women are more careful of their speech habits, inclined, say some scholars, to stick to standard usage, avoiding the "unacceptable" in vocabulary and grammar. Caution is a way of avoiding prejudice and maintaining status. So it seems that men invent the slang, unafraid of substandard usage or unconventional structure.

It is probably true that women are much more inclined to use "tag questions." "We had a good time, didn't we?" "That will be fun, won't it?" "Well, I tried, didn't I?" We hear a special pitch pattern here: The pitch of the last two words goes down and then up, an appeal for support and agreement. Is it only women who, when listening attentively, cock the head on one side? Sociologists suggest that this is a posture of subservience, perhaps even a presentation position.

A woman's vocal cords are shorter than a man's, resulting in a higher pitch of the voice. Does this fact militate against the right and proper assertion of authority by women? Is it true that women newscasters intentionally lower their voices on the air so as to match more nearly the pitch of their male associates? In this connection, note how much attention is given to a female voice that has a distinctly lower pitch, such as that of Tallulah Bankhead or Lauren Bacall.

In ancient Rome women's words were restricted. They were allowed to swear by only one of the Heavenly Twins Castor and Pollux. *Ecastor!* they could say. Men could invoke either one (*edepol!*). In our culture we have similar restrictions. Women are not supposed to use obscene words that are common to the speech of men.

In several Asian cultures women were (are) required to walk behind their men. Those who have read Vergil's *Aeneid* will recall that Aeneas's wife, Creusa, followed him as they tried to escape from Troy. She could not walk alongside and so more easily was lost. This position is, of course, a signal of subservience.

But far less clear is the pervading degradation of women in our language. The opposite of male ought, by its derivation, to be

MEANING, MESSAGE, AND METAPHOR
91

something like *femelle* (as it is in French). But we have made the feminine over so that it appears to be simply, not a distinct person, but some sort of male: a fe-male.

In contrast to the long list of derogatory terms for women, there are few similar terms restricted to men, although some of them may occasionally be used for women. We always think of males when we use the terms *bum, wino, drifter, lush.*

It was Vergil, again, who described woman as *varium et muta-bile semper*, "always unstable and changeable." To add to this insult, he made the adjective neuter "always an unstable thing." English cannot reproduce the subtle insinuation of these neuter adjectives. The duke in *Rigoletto* tells us the same thing: "*La dònna è mobile.*"

34
For an Equal Lefts Amendment

Anyone who is left-handed or who has left-handers in the family knows the troubles the left-hander has, troubles caused by a society that is determinedly right-handed. Such troubles are not limited to the locations of levers, handles, controls on adding machines, telephones, TV or radio sets, or the obscuring of the values of playing cards. They go much deeper, thanks to our language.

Unfortunately the words *right* and *left* have many other associations. We put *right* before *left* in lists. But when describing foolishness, we put them the other way around: He scattered his money *left* and *right*. All sorts of splendid things are *right*. Justice, morality are right; you must get things right or set them right. Your best friend is your right-hand man or woman (and might well be so, for you need someone on that side to protect you; your shield, of course, is held on the left arm because you, of course, are right-handed). The cry may be "Right on!" The Right Bower in cards out-ranks the Left. The place of honor is at the host's right.

Compare the use of *left*. A left-handed compliment is not a compliment at all, and a left-handed marriage is no marriage. Evil omens were supposed to come from the left. The Greek word *aris-teros* (left) is of uncertain origin, but meant "ill-omened."

Latin is no exception. *Dexter* means "right, right hand." So the dexterous person is, naturally, right-handed and so, skilled. If one is ambidextrous, one has two right hands, the left evidently having been trained to operate as a right. In French, *droit* means "right(hand)." So if you are adroit, you are simply right-handed.

Latin is worse, if anything, because *sinister*, which means "left-hand," in English has dreadful synonyms: dire, baleful, malign. A youngster once asked why an old maid is called a "sinister." Such is the extent of prejudice! Superstition or just plain ignorance about the left has sometimes forced left-handers to write with the right hand, causing serious troubles.

However, the left-hander is not always at a disadvantage. Al-though a baseball diamond is set up for right-handed infielders (and so it should be because there are so many more of them), a left-hander at first base is a real asset for he is ready to throw to any base after catching a ball. Lefties are in demand to bat and are es-sential on a pitching staff. A soccer team must have left-footed kickers. A left-handed tennis player may cause problems for oppo-nents.

In the automobile of most countries, the "four-on-the-floor" gearshift is for right-handers; and so are sundry gadgets, the auto-matic gearshift lever, for example.

Let the right-hander try operating a telephone or cutting a piece of paper with the left hand. Fortunately, companies manufac-ture things for left-handers, including scissors and belt buckles.

35
The Size of It

Like the left-handers, the "smalls," people who have comparatively small bodies and are below average height, suffer handicaps and discriminations. The tall one gets the job in competition with an equally well-qualified short person. Women who are quite short may wear high heels when going for an interview.

Indeed, virtually all the arguments offered for considerate treatment of minorities may be just as well advanced for smalls. How about a Dean of Smalls in a college? Pictures are hung, telephones placed on the wall, notices displayed on the bulletin board to suit the average height. As to modern basketball, even a person of average height is out.

Like *right* and *left*, *big* and *little* carry connotations that favor the former and demean the latter. "It was a *small* thing for him to do." In other words, it was mean. "Be *big* about this; don't be *small*." Here are loaded words.

We do much better in our handy euphemisms for *fat* and *skinny*. We can say *stout* and *slender*. There is no refuge from *big* and *little*. Thus, though the tall person has some problems, he or she is likely to be looked up to figuratively as well as literally.

36
The Ups and Downs of Meanings

Many words start out with a "neutral" meaning, such as Latin *villanus*, which meant simply "a farmer, one who lives in a villa." It suffered "pejoration," a fine Latin word about equal to English "worsening." Not every farmer is wicked, but a villain certainly is. French has not taken this word all the way down; *vilain* means "ugly."

Critic goes back to Greek *krinein*, "to choose." Thus a critic is one who is supposed to make a choice, be it good or bad, and a critical situation is one in which a choice has to be made. Moreover, a critique of a work ought to be an evaluation of it. But critics are so often censorious, so often ready to condemn a book or a play or anything else, that criticism usually implies an unfavorable judgment, and to be critical of something is most often to object to it. Such has been the pejoration of a once-neutral word. A *valet* was originally an attendant upon someone. Its precise origin is not known. Today it refers to a servant. French made it over into *varlet*, and we use that word. It means a scoundrel.

In Latin, a *pagus* is simply a district, countryside. Thus to the urbane (Latin *urbanus*, from *urbem*, city) a *paganus* was an "outsider," and therefore inferior, a *pagan*. The word today refers to anyone who is not a member of any organized religion, in short, a *heathen*. So much for someone who lives "outside." Latin *librum*, "book," has a diminutive, *libellum*, meaning "small book, short note." Now it may mean a lawsuit. *Odor* and *smell* might be regarded as meaning the same sort of thing. But if we say, "Something smells around here," we have another instance of pejoration.

In Greek, an *idiotes* was simply a private citizen, from *idios*, "one's own." Thus an *idiom* is a language's way of saying things. But

MEANING, MESSAGE, AND METAPHOR

an individual way often seems odd to other people. So we have arrived at the meaning of *idiot* as a stupid person, whereas *idiosyncracy* may be an oddity without a negative meaning.

In German, *Knabe* means "boy." Some boys are bad, and so they are *knaves*. In a deck of cards, pejoration has been halted. The *Jack* is often called a *knave* (especially in Britain), and it means no more than "boy."

Latin *experiri* means "to try." Ex-*peri*-ment is a trial, and a *periculum* was also a trial. But many a trial is dangerous, so that this word came to mean "danger," and from it we have English *peril*. But there is more to this story. From the same origin is the word *pirate* which comes from Greek. Originally, a pirate was an entrepreneur, ready to try something. Pirates went downhill and so did the word.

Latin *plausus* meant simply "applause." But a *plausible* explanation of something is convincing, worthy of *plaudits*.

Latin *pius* meant "conscientious, dutiful." But today it may imply ostentatious devoutness. *Wretch* comes from a root *wreg-* which means "shove, push." So an unfortunate wretch is someone who has been pushed around. The word today often has a pejorative meaning, implying much more than does wretched.

Anglo-Saxon *hus-wif*, "housewife," has also given us a much-deteriorated *hussy*.

But not every word has gone downhill. The Anglo-Saxon word *sty-ward*, "one who guards the pig sty," is now the dignified *steward*, and the *loaf-ward*, "one who guards the bread," is now the lofty *lord* of the manor. A *comes stabuli*, "companion of the stable," is now a constable.

Latin *caballus* was a slang word for "horse." It won out over the standard *equus*, and from it we get French *cheval*, Spanish *caballo*. A man on a horse, then, is a *chevalier* or a *caballero*. If your local knight treats you well, he is chivalrous. If he is haughty and brusque, then he is treating you in a cavalier fashion.

Hard to believe is that the word *glamour* comes from *grammar*. Glamour was originally associated with charm, attraction. But it later came to mean magic with which learning was associated, and the term *grammar* had a general meaning of learning. This is a hard pill to swallow, but a dictionary is likely to attest to it.

Almost as extreme is the development of the Greek word *ther*, "wild animal." From it came *theriakon*, "pertaining to a wild beast." The next step was to use the word for a remedy for a bite of a wild beast ("wild-beast stuff"). Then it was applied to any remedy. Since medicines often taste bad, it was sweetened, and after that, was used for sweet substances, and it is now with us as *treacle*, which used to mean a medical compound, but now refers to any sweet substance.

Paradise in Greek was just a "park." Words associated with the church have often been "ennobled" as this was. Latin *pastor* means simply "shepherd," and *Bible* is from Greek for "book." Latin *scriptura* referred to anything written; now it refers to "Sacred Writ."

Sometimes a word retains its original meaning in one form and a pejorative in another. Thus from Latin *potare*, "drink," we get both *potion* and *poison*. *Tradere*, "to hand over," gives us *tradition*, a handing over of customs, and *treason*, handing over a country. *Inequities*, from Latin for "not equal," should be corrected, but *iniquities* are far worse.

37
What's in a Name?

In addition to the names we give living creatures, we have a remarkable number of names for groups of them. Well enough known are a *herd* of elephants, a *pack* of hounds. Less common are a *pride* of lions, a *sloth* of bears.

James Lipton, in *An Exaltation of Larks*, lists terms for groups used in old-time hunting. The term should contain some suggestion of an activity or a characteristic of the animal; hence his use of *exaltation* for the lark. Anyone who has been fortunate enough to see and hear a lark would agree that it is appropriate for that blithe spirit, singing at Heaven's gate. In Lipton's book we find a *parliament* of owls, a *skulk* of foxes, a *knot* of toads, all accompanied by ingenious and remarkable illustrations.

Reading this book encourages one to make up other special names. Why not a *stolidity* of frumps, a *drooling* of voyeurs, a *polysyllabification* of professors of education, and, with a pun from the Greek, a *galaxy* of milk maids (Greek for "milky circle"). Additional suggestions are an *insinuation* of ferrets, a *shrinking* of psychiatrists, a *column* of accountants, and a *scurrying* of commuters.

Observe that there is no group word for the cat, for cats do not operate in groups; they are on their own.

38
What Do Animals Say?

Speakers of any language make over "foreign" sounds they hear into their own sound pattern. They do so with animal cries which turn up quite differently in various languages.

The French dog is supposed to say "ouah, ouah" whereas ours say "woof, woof." Orphan Annie's dog in the cartoon says "arf." A drawing on a Greek vase shows two dogs facing one another. Beneath them are the letters *BAU, BAU*. The Greeks seem to have heard their dogs as we do.

We claim that our ducks say "quack, quack." If they go to France, they will have to learn to say "couin, couin." German roosters say "kikeriki;" the French, "cocorico." As for our own, they are credited with "cock-a-doodle-doo." At least all three languages agree on assigning the roosters four or more syllables; and indeed, that is what we hear in a barnyard.

Our turkeys say "gobble, gobble," and that seems a bit better

"The name that springs to the mind at a time like this is Joyce Kilmer."

than the French "glou, glou." The French pig says "gron, gron." As for ours, someone, for some reason, recorded pig noises and found that if there is one thing our pigs do not say, it is "oink."

Now as to the cat: it naturally has nothing to do with all this fol-de-rol of this animal saying this and that animal saying that, depending on location. German cats, French cats, Latin cats of old, and cats in our country today simply said and say "meow." Characteristically, unlike lesser creatures who must say things more than once in order to get attention, they say it once, not twice.

> The Cat, with mind inscrutable,
> Maintains "meow" immutable.
> That noise is heard in every nation
> Without a single meow-tation.
> Where'er it be, what e'er its name,
> The cat's "meow" remains the same.

39
Talking by Type and Signs

Humans communicate through the spoken language, to be sure; and perhaps only one percent of communication is through the written word. But there are many other ways to communicate. To many the following symbols will be easily understood:

"$-- \quad --- \quad .-. \quad ... \quad . \quad -.-. \quad --- \quad -.. \quad .$"

These dots and dashes say "Morse code," a system of signals that usually comes by ear. We can also signal by flashing a beam of light, a longer flash representing a dash, a shorter one, a dot, when the signals come by eye.

We can use two flags which, by their positions, represent the letters of the alphabet, the semaphore system, when again the signals come by eye.

Relatively few people used these methods, but in our communication system signaling by type plays an IMPORTANT part.

In our use of capital letters, we capitalize the adjectives that refer to countries or to people, the English language, a French professor. But the French and Italians do not do so: *la langue anglaise, un professeur français; la lingua inglese, un professore francese.* Germans begin nouns with a capital letter. Thus *Tannenbaum* may be a man's name, or it may mean a fir tree, and only the context tells which. Capital letters are useful. When reading, we can see the difference between *march* and *March.* We may write, "Mars and Earth are planets," using capitals. But we do not use a capital when we write, "Where on earth have you been?"

Hyphens often help to represent intonations of speech. For example, "He gave out five dollar bills" or "He gave out five-dollar bills." We hear the difference when these two sentences are pronounced. Compare "It is a long-lost poem" with "It is a long lost poem." The hyphen tells us that the poem has been lost for a long time and does not tell us whether it is long or short. The second tells us that it is long, but not how long it has been lost. Our speech pattern signals the difference.

Type signals give us information in the following passage (written in the "indeed he" style): "On a dark November evening in the year 189–, a figure, muffled in a greatcoat, might have been seen mounting the steps of No. —— Berkeley Square. 'D——n,' said Lord Fafnir of Dragonwyck (for it was indeed he), 'I've lost my key!'"

The dash in the date and the house number protect the author from a suit for libel by some litigious resident of the Square. The dashes in d——n are supposed to soothe Aunt Tillie's sensibilities, even though she knows d——n well what the word is.

See the effect of two question marks instead of one: "Do you believe that??" Obviously anyone who writes this does not believe it and clearly informs the reader of the fact.

Parentheses signal that supplementary information is being supplied, and one who is reading aloud will respond to the signal and read in a lower pitch and more rapidly what is in them, as in "Joe (he's the fellow I told you about) came to see me."

The floating comma, otherwise called the apostrophe, serves a number of purposes as a signal. It marks the loss of letters. In *I've*, the loss of *ha*; in *don't*, an *o*; in *we're*, an *a*; in *it's*, an *i*; and *wi* or *sha* in *I'll*. It tells the reader the difference between two sentences that sound the same: "the sailor's home" and "the sailors' home." "We saw the directors' clean house" tells us that mops and brooms had been at work. "We saw the directors clean house" indicates that some people were fired.

Sometimes we find the apostrophe where it does not belong. "Make sure all cable's are disconnected." This may be the hoisting of a tribute to Miss Fidditch, who harped on the apostrophe. We sometimes see the same thing in "Closed Sunday's." The usual parking-lot admonition has no apostrophe; but some indicate that one person owns all the cars: "Cars towed at owner's expense."

Quotation marks (which the British call "inverted commas" even though only one pair in today's type is upside down) may send a signal of irony: Who is this "leader" they are sending us? They may serve a newspaper as legal protection: The "burglar" was locked up. Or they may call attention to some special meaning: It was a sort of "farewell" party.

A colon can replace them in newspaper headlines to save space: JONES: CONGRESS MUST ACT.

We use special type for special signals. Agatha Christie's Miss Marple might say, "Why is everything always carried *into* that house and nothing *out of* it?" The italics show the stress put on contrasting words. By an interesting "back formation" we say that one who is constantly stressing words speaks *in italics*. Just so, in headlines, the bigger the type, the louder the signal, so that we say, "The headlines screamed."

The asterisk (*) served in the 1950 edition of Eric Partridge's *A Dictionary of Slang and Unconventional Usage* to soothe the censor by being inserted for one letter in the traditional "four-letter words." The asterisks are not to be seen in the 1970 edition. *Tempora mutantur!*

So-called leader dots may signal an omission in a quotation. "When . . . it becomes necessary . . . to dissolve the bonds . . . ." Dots at the end of a sentence can signal the trailing away of a voice: "Well, I don't know about that . . . ." Or, for another effect: "Down he sank, down . . . down . . . down."

Brackets set off something an editor or writer has inserted. "These times [the 1960s] were dangerous." Or, quoting a mistake: "The vase fell off the mantle [*sic*]."

The writing of the exclamation *O* with a single letter lends special flavor:

Sail on, O Ship of State!
Sail on, O Union, strong and great!

To write *Oh* here would take all the wind out of Longfellow's sails.

We may say of *O*:

Its firm and smooth rotundity
Infuses deep profundity
Inevitably solemn.

Authors often use incorrect spelling to signal a lack of education in some character. Thus when the old cowhand says, "Do we hafta have wimmin around here?" the author tells us that he would probably pronounce *hafta* and *wimmin* that way and the spelling represents the sounds. Note the change in the final consonant of *have* in "hafta."

As to the word *have*, think of a learner of our English language who hasta [*sic*] cope with "The superintendent *has* been visiting frequently, so the teacher *has had* to *have* the pupils *have* their work ready."

Advertisements show the many ways in which type can be used for effect. The ampersand (&) gives "class" to the titles of firms.

The ampersand lends glamour
To a name like Jones & Hammer,
Typographically fancy.

Ampersand stands for "and per se and," that is, "and of itself and."

40
Making Up Names

The naivete of native speakers about their language is seen in the names assigned by various writers to "other-world" beings in their stories. William Blake (1757–1827) created such names as Ahamia, Urizen, Urthona, all supposed to sound exotic. Yet the sound patterns here are all purely English. Tolkien in our times made up Frodo, Bilbo Baggins, Gandalf. *Star Wars* produced Darth Vader, Obi-Wan Kenobi, Han Solo. Every one of these names consists of ordinary English sounds. Authors, quite understandably, have no idea of how the sound pattern of one tongue differs from that of all others. If they want their characters to be different, then their speech must also be. They make up queer creatures, queer ideas, queer customs, but make noises that are all-English. *Watership Down* (1974) by Richard G. Adams provides a mild exception. Here some characters have names that begin with /h/ + /l/ and /h/ + /r/, a bold step toward suggesting an exotic speech.

The thing to do is to have some visitors from outer space whose sound pattern, not just vocabulary, is entirely non-English. Within the following non-English consonant clusters, we can insert non-English vowels. Out of the space ship comes a being who says, "Me *Mgobj*," and pointing to his friend, "Her *Zbothd*. We from

Planet *Pfauh*; our ship called *Ptukch*. Take us to your *Kmily*." No English words either begin or end with the consonants in these names.

The British changed "Infanta de Castile" into "Elephant and Castle," the name of the underground station in London. French *chartreuse* turns up as Charterhouse.

Catchy names, easy to say, have a power of their own, especially in advertising. Some have come into the public domain, for example, *frigidaire*, which the British turn into *fridge*.

Automobile models are given names of animals whose fine characteristics are supposed to suggest something fine about the car itself. But manufacturers are running out of catchy names, so here are some suggestions:

How about *Quagga*, a sturdy, four-footed (four-wheel drive) creature with a "good" sound. Never mind that it is "a striped ass resembling a donkey." Nobody will look it up. Slogan: "Load the family into your Quagga-Wagon and wow the neighbors with its luxury look." Why not *Yak* also for a four-wheel drive? The name suggests a powerful no-nonsense animal, a hard worker. "We back our Yak against all comers." *Zebu* should be a zinger. On TV, the usual flowing-haired damsel with flowing robe, nestling up to her Zebu, saying, "Eet ees ze supair carr, ze zoom zoom Zebu six." Nor should the Italian word *Zingara*, "gypsy," be overlooked. "Yield to the gypsy in you. Cast off care, and zing away in your zippy Zingara *dee-lucks* sports car."

Novelists have enjoyed making up suggestive names for their characters, and no one was better at it than Dickens. Wackford Squeers has an unforgettable ring, reminding us of the creature so named. Martin Chuzzlewit and Noddy Boffin belong here, as does Shakespeare's Sir Toby Belch.

"What's in a name? That which we call a rose . . . ." There is a great deal in a name, and in these days of the media belittling people, the old saw must be revised:

Sticks and stones may break my bones,
But calling names can destroy me utterly.

Who, even among the most ardent of Nazis, could have cried, "Heil Schickelgruber," without laughing. The Italians did not have to change any name, for *duce*, "leader," was ready to hand, and troops of soldiers chanted "Duce, Duce," a chant to rouse the people for Mussolini.

Consider the changes made in the names of actors to provide easy and pleasant sounds. Issur Danielovitch turned up, to the admiration and enjoyment of moviegoers, as Kirk Douglas. Veronica Lake rather than Constance Ockelman appeared on the marquee, and millions mourned the death of immensely popular Marion Morrison, a.k.a. John Wayne.

Let the next group of invaders come with true, exotic names, and do not let them point with the finger. Only a minority on earth do that.

41
Old Saws Resharpened

Many an old saw or proverb can be reversed to good effect. When is "topsy-turvy" "hunky-dory"? Thus, for example, we change "Procrastination is the thief of time" into "Punctuality is the thief of time." ("We'll just wait a few minutes until the rest get here.")

A *proverb* is a saying that expresses a well-known truth. A *maxim* sets forth in capsule form some basic principle, often dealing with conduct. It gets its name from Latin *maxima propositio*, "a very important proposal." It came to us by way of French, dropping its noun en route.

What is a *motto*? The word goes back by way of Italian to Latin *muttire*, "mutter." A motto is a phrase or sentence that sets forth an ideal or a goal. We can deal with all of these phenomena at once, for they are all subject to reversals and revisions.

It is so true that "honor is without profit in your own country" that even a prophet would agree. "Where there's a will there's an heir" is a commonplace, but how about "Great aches from little toe corns grow"? "Speech is silver, but silence is rare" speaks to the constant yammering on TV and radio.

It was John Heywood (1497–1580) who said, "One swallow maketh not a summer," and he is usually misquoted. It can be revised to "One swallow maketh not a drunk." It was Heywood, too, who said, "Many hands make light werke." In some cases, many hands often make light work more difficult ("Please, mother, I'd rather do it myself").

If we may use jack to mean money, we turn "All work and no play makes Jack a dull boy" into "All work and no play makes jack," or "All jack and no work makes a dull playboy."

The name of Richard Franck (1624–1708) is not likely to spring to the mind in connection with anything. But he gave us two popular sayings in one sentence: "Art imitates nature, and necessity is the mother of invention." We have heard the former turned around many times. But it is the latter that tells a true tale in reverse: "Invention is the mother of necessity." Invent telephones, TV, or automobiles, and everybody has to have one.

If we consider that certain activities are associated with certain groups, we may say, "Too many crooks spoil the brothel." Tight-fitting sweaters are designed to "pull your eyes over the wool;" and it might be that your "cook has just been goosed."

Maxims, which the Romans called *sententiae*, have a familiar and timely sound in a collection made by Publilius Syrus, a Roman freedman. He berates the rich as heartily as does the Bible, as he moralizes about misers. English follows the lead of Syrus and the Latin language; for Latin *miser* means "miserable." It was clear in those days that anyone who counts his *pelf*, or who has pelf to count, must be wretched. *Pelf*, by the way, has the same root as *pilfer*; so our miser's money has been stolen, too.

Here are some of Syrus's sayings:

A miser is his own worst enemy.

Expect from others what you have done to them.

A miser does nothing right except when he dies.

One who helps nobody has no right to ask for help.

It is the judge who is condemned when a guilty man goes free.

Anyone who gets shipwrecked a second time has no business blaming Neptune.

A sick man had better not make his doctor his heir.

You find out who your friends are when trouble comes.

What good is money if you can't use it?

An irate parent is cruelest to himself.

Give anybody more than he ought to have, and he will ask for more.

He gives twice who gives quickly.

After all, many a jest is spoken in truth, and Syrus shows us that people are people, no matter where you find them.

One number turns up in all sorts of sayings: forty. Ali Baba had to deal with forty thieves. We "catch forty winks." An old description of tousled hair was "It stood up forty ways for Sunday." Napoleon, about to invade Egypt, said to his soldiers, "From the summit of yonder pyramids, forty centuries look down upon you."

The age of forty has long been regarded as an important point in life. In *The Maiden Queen* (3.1) Dryden writes, "I am resolved to grow fat and look young till forty." Wordsworth in *The Cock Is Crowing* says, "The cattle are grazing . . . there are forty feeding like one."

So the number is proverbial and finds its way into ceremonial customs. Before Buddhist burial services can be performed, the ashes of the deceased must wait for forty days. July 15 is St. Swithin's Day, when the weather tells us what to expect for the next forty days.

Perhaps the oddest use of this number is found in the number of days for which patients with various diseases (e.g., scarlet fever) used to be isolated: forty days, and the very word *quarantine* is from Italian *quaranta*, "forty." Did medics of old really know what the right length of time was, or did they simply fix on that famous symbol of "a long time"?

In the Bible we often find this number: Genesis 7:4, "I will cause it to rain upon the earth for forty days." Exodus 16:35, "The children of Israel did eat manna forty years." Exodus 24:18, "Moses was on the mountain forty days and forty nights." Numbers 13:25, "They returned from searching the land after forty days." 1 Samuel 17:16, "The Philistine presented himself for forty days." 1 Kings 19:8, "Elijah arose and went forty days and forty nights unto Horeb." Matthew 4:2, Jesus "fasted forty days and forty nights" (and so Lent lasts for forty days). Deuteronomy 25:3, "Forty stripes may he give him, and not exceed."

42
Educanto or Pedaguese

The following statement came from a Department of Communications of a university. It is a fine example of the jargon, call it Educanto or Pedaguese as you will, in which "educators" talk to each other: "Communicologists (what a word!) have attempted to cull the various perspectives to synthesize salient concepts into an integrated framework." Who among us mere mortals could cull a perspective? Or synthesize a concept? It continues: "Scholars [?] have established a distinctive field of communication research with a multi-theoretical delineation of parameters and general orientations." Would you like to be able to delineate a parameter; and could you do it multi-theoretically?

The following unbelievable statement appeared in an "educational" periodical: "If a student is to become proficient in history, algebra or reading, he must encounter these subjects and be led to make reaction to them." Could anyone have written that? You have to encounter a subject and be led to make a reaction. What sort of nonsense is this? The article continues: "To bring about these [*sic*] results, the teacher should have some knowledge of the subject he teaches, and be willing to entertain the basic ideas in the subject." To suggest that a teacher should know something about the subject is certainly a radical idea. How one entertains ideas, the author does not say, but goes on: "It is true, of course, that teachers who are lacking in knowledge of their subject can arrange for necessary stimulation by using other resources or by various indirect means." This writer is a realist, anyway, who knows that some teachers are ill prepared, and urges them to be frauds, too, by faking their way along, arranging for "stimulation" the while. Yet anyone who knows anything about young people knows that they can spot a phony in less time than it takes to talk about "making a reaction." But there is more: "Little will be said [by whom or where?] about just how much the teacher should know about his subject. For day-in-day-out teaching, it would be helpful if he knew as much as his best pupil is likely to learn, and prudence calls for a comfortable margin beyond this." Prudence must know, as we do, that this statement represents a total abandonment of any pretense to learning or scholarship. It is, in short, outrageous.

A high school principal recently said, in public, "I am apologizing to the faculty via my own volition and by no method of prompting. I adhere to the dictum that professionalism must be maintained at all costs, and by no means would I thrust any aspect of our profession which may be construed as negative." No method of prompting, I am sure, would induce any of us to thrust around an aspect, even via our own volition.

A college in the West, worried about faculty voting, published the following statement: "Concern for the need [how about the need for concern?] to facilitate a more helpful acceptance orientated vehicle as antecedent provision to voting." In order to vote, it seems, you have to have a vehicle; and when is a provision not antecedent?

A college president said, of efforts to balance the budget, "We will divert the force of this fiscal stress into leverage energy and pry important budgetary consideration and control out of the fiscal and administrative procedures." Would you buy a diploma from this man?

A school superintendent upon taking office said that he had his "prioricities." He did not go into specificities, but he might have referred, as did a college dean, to "the purposes animating my endeavors." An animated endeavor must be an awesome thing, but it might "create a public foment," as a publication of a state department of education once warned. Another such statement said that some urban school districts might fall into irretrievable depths. How does one go about retrieving a depth? What do you do with it when you have it?

Participants at a meeting of educators were promised "two program tracks which will emphasize the presentation of factual material within a workshop setting." As he was a-setting in a workshop setting, one participant wrote:

There's two-way traffic on them two tracks,
A-comin' and a-goin' an' presentin' true facks.

Even the scientific folk get infected. An advertisement invited applicants with "strong personal skills as they would interface broadly within the development function."

One professor of "education" speaks highly of "operationalizing coping skills," and another said his students had "a full array of competence." People who come under the influence of those who write so atrociously may themselves be poisoned and infect others. How can the writers of Educanto be stopped? Apparently, they cannot, but their writings can be held up to the scorn and contempt of all who believe in the majesty of the English language and who understand the damage done by its misuse.

E. B. White once said that, although English is a splendid language, it can "throw whoever leaps cocksurely into the saddle."* The untutored and unwary should not monkey with Great Big

* E. B. White, *The Second Tree from the Corner* (New York: Harper & Brothers, 1954), 166.

Words. One critic said of a portrait of George Washington that it was "the most literal similitude" he had ever seen. A manufacturer of an airplane advertised it as first-rate in "crashability," and a beer was promoted for its "drinkability."

Even the personnel in the office are guilty. One inter-office memo, replying to a management request that idle chitchat be reduced, said, "This would lead to an oppressive office climate and thwart self-actualization and the emergence of vital leader-subordinate relationship." After all, what are you doing in an office if not working hard to self-actualize yourself? One corporation commented on its grisly "bottom-line" figure as follows: "Recurring incidents generated an adverse impact on company operations." Such obscure writing comes close to being an effort to mislead the public.

A banker, asked whether a certain loan would be renewed, said, "I would not come to a conclusion in terms of what we could or could not do." He who reads this could come to a conclusion not to do business with that banker.

A hospital press release about a patient said, "He is experiencing difficulty in mobility." In this kind of jargon, you cannot "have" anything, you must experience it. "The patient is experiencing tuberculosis"?

A cereal manufacturer said, "The 18-to–50-year old segment of the population is the least consumptive." He just couldn't say right out that people in this age range eat less.

A TV station, trying to avoid controversy, announced: "There was a minimal correlation . . . between priority social issue and station priority."

That the virus of Educanto is not confined to this side of the water is proved by the following, which was published in the *London Daily Telegraph* on 25 May 1979: "The scenic quality of the coastline of South East Devon is evaluated by using a bipolar semantic differential test developed from personal construct theory. The varying response of groups of operators to the scenery is discussed in relation to physical attributes, and cliff heights and beach character are seen to influence scenic quality significantly quanti-

"Are you ready to implement your obligations to identify the wishes, desires, expectations of this woman in the context of an interpersonal relationship?"

fied." Why should there always be an England if it harbors anyone on its shores who writes such nonsense? One feature of this type of writing may protect the one who writes it because the passive voice is constantly used: "It is thought that," "It has been discovered that." The writer puts no finger on any one person. The passive voice is the preferred resort of the ineffective and incompetent writer.

PART SIX
FUN WITH WORDS

43
The Last Word in Dictionaries

Just for fun, let us look at the last word listed under each letter in a large-sized dictionary. (*Aardvark*, long touted as the first word in a dictionary is, of course, by no means the first, because we have many words spelled simply with *A*.)

Azyme, czarism, and *nytril* will do for a sampling. But they are not remarkable.

A *qutb* was an Icelandic saint; *myzus* is a genus of aphids; and *jynx* a genus of woodpeckers. Under *H* we find *hythergraph*, a device for recording temperature and rainfall.

In early times, the national militia of England was called by a most unwarlike word: *fyrd*. It might have been called upon to protect a *pyx-jury*, as for assayed coins, perhaps on a *tzut*, a brightly patterned square of cotton.

A *byzen* is a disgraceful spectacle. Persons responsible might be shackled in *gyves*, and fed only *uzarin*, the active principle of the uzara root.

Kyte refers to the bowel or stomach, a *lyta* is a cartilaginous strip under an animal's tongue, and a *xyster* is a surgical instrument for scraping bones.

Syzygy, the point of opposition or conjunction with the sun, is required for total eclipses.

The *wyvern* is a mythical dragon seen nowadays only in heraldic signs. It might take shelter under a *xystus*, a portico, where a *y-worm* might be living.

Ozotype, a carbon process, might be *vying* for last place under the *O*'s with *Ozymandian*, and would win, because we cannot allow proper names in this list.

An upstanding citizen might pay bills with *eyrir*, an Icelandic monetary unit, and at the same time maintain *izzat*, Hindi for "personal dignity." At your local zoo, look for a *rytina* which is the Steller's sea cow. At a lab, researchers might employ *czapedox*, "a culture for fungi."

Smaller dictionaries used to end with *zymurgy*, which is nothing more than fermentation. But the majestic word *zyzzogeton*, "leaf-hopper," replaced it and heralded The End. Then came the Random House Dictionary with Laurence Urdang's *zzz*, "the sound of a snore."

Proper names are tempting, for example, *Mzabite* (Berber), *Tzutuhil* (a people of Guatemala), or *Dzungaria* (a vast arid region of northwestern China).

44
Pangrams and the Alphabet

A sentence that contains all the letters of an alphabet can be called a *pangram* (Greek for "every letter"). It ought to have as few letters as possible and make sense.

The best known is "The quick brown fox jumps over the lazy dog." It contains 35 letters for an alphabet of 26; so it is only 74 percent efficient. Changing the first word to *A* brings the percentage up to 79.

We can get down to 32 letters (81 percent) and a hearty ring to it in "Pack my box with five dozen liquor jugs."

Here are three tries, each with 31 letters (84 percent): "Quick brave dogs jump the lazy wan fox," "Jackdaws love my big sphinx of quartz," and "Quip whiz Jack moved fast to grab lynx." With but 29 letters (89.7 percent) we can wrestle with "Quick wafting zephyrs vex bold Jim." With only 28, try this one (93 percent): "Waltz, nymph, for quick jigs vex Bud."

The best French pangram I know is, "*Comptez les verres de whisky fangeux que je bois.*" ("Count the glasses of muddy whisky that I drink.") *Whisky* is valuable because it is in itself 100 percent efficient, yielding six letters with no repeats. Much better for English is *facetiously*, which has eleven different letters. Note that it has only four syllables, the first and third with the same vowel sounds, and the second and fourth with the same diphthong. It does contain, in alphabetical order, five letters which we use to represent various kinds of vowel sounds. But these are letters not vowels.

I composed my own Latin pangram: *Qvid picus Karthagini mox flebit?* which contains 28 letters for the 21 in the Latin alphabet (75 percent efficient). The translation is "What will the woodpecker be complaining about in Carthage?" Never mind asking why a woodpecker should act so; the sentences we find in elementary textbooks are just as ridiculous. I recall one in a Latin text: "The soldier wounded the horse's head with a spear." What sort of barbaric business is this? Mark Twain called attention to foolish sentences, claiming that his German book asked him to translate "The bird is waiting in the blacksmith's shop on account of the rain."

The Latin alphabet, by the way, has no *J*. That letter developed from a "long-tailed" *I*, and is used to represent a consonant (Latin uses *I* for both vowel and consonant). It has no *W*, representing /w/ by the letter *V*. The consonant /v/ is not in Latin. Latin has no *Y* or *Z* either, these letters having been imported and put at the end of the alphabet to stand for Greek sounds not heard in Latin. Greek *zeta*, which provided the *Z*, is the sixth letter in the Greek alphabet, and *upsilon*, which provided the *Y*, is the twentieth.

Imagine the delight of an audience at a meeting of teachers of Latin and Greek, when a school superintendent, praising a fine teacher, said, "He knew his Greek from *alpha* to *zeta*." All hands present hoped the teacher would eventually advance down the alphabet to a triumphant *omega*.

Q, *X*, and *K* are useless letters in the Roman alphabet, and useless in English, too. The Greek *Xi* (written *X*) stands fourteenth in the Greek alphabet, and was in early times added at the end of the standard Latin alphabet, a useless appendage. But Greek words use this letter, even begin words with it, and it has proved confusing. Many people, when confronted with the name *Xavier*, do not know that we pronounce it as though it began with /z/. Instead, they sound out the name of our letter *X*, and say, "Eks-avier." Yet these same folk have no trouble with *Xerox* or *xylophone*.

The same saint's name appears in Spanish as *Javier*, and base-ball commentators have learned to treat it as starting with /h/. But they are not so skilled when it comes to *San Juan*, because the second word comes out as /wan/, instead of /hwan/. *Xavier* in Italian, by the way, is *Saverio*.

45
Waiting for the Train, Plane, Bus, or Space Shuttle

What to do till the plane leaves? The Word Watcher will be able to while away the time with any number of things, because, as the professor of education put it, "he possesses a full array of competence."

Start with an easy one: make a list of common expressions that contain a set of three elements: *hook, line, and sinker; faith, hope, and love; men, women, and children.* Here, as with many such games, if several people are on hand, points can be awarded to anyone who has a set that nobody else has thought of.

Think of unusual consonant clusters, such as words that have the sequence *ckg* in their spelling, *backgammon*, for example. Why not invent useful words with this feature, such as *snackgrabber* (a pig at a picnic). *Blackguard* is too easy.

Try for words in which writing a letter twice produces an entirely different word. For instance, *rifle/riffle* or *filing/filling*. (*Rifle* in the sense of plundering or stealing is from the same source as *riffle*. But *rifle*, the gun, is not.)

Important in English grammar is the stress accent which distinguishes the nouns *CON-tract* and *PER-mit* from the verbs *con-TRACT* and *per-MIT*. Notable exception: *cement*, which is accented the same for both noun and verb.

How many sets of four homonyms can be found? Examples: *rite, wright, right, write*; or *sear, sere, seer, cere* (shroud for a coffin).

Make up new names for groups of people: a *blunder of baserunners, a crush of shoppers, a lurching of lushes.*

Anagrams can be amusing. Perhaps the most famous is formed from the question asked by Pontius Pilate: *Quid est veritas?* The anagram answer was *Est vir qui adest.* (What is the truth? It is the man who is here.) It is surprising that the four letters of the Latin word *amor* (love) can be rearranged to form six more Latin words: *armo* (arm, equip), *mora* (delay), *ramo* (branch), *oram* (seacoast), *Roma* (Rome), and *Maro* (Vergil's family name). As if these were not enough, they also give us *roam* and *Omar*.

Often claimed as English words that have no rhymes are *months, eighths, twelfths.* Try to find some. What rhymes with *tufts* or *bulbs*?

How many words can be found that refer to only one gender? After using up family relations (*aunt/uncle*, etc.) put down pairs such as *bull/cow, fox/vixen.* There are at least fifty such pairs. Whose list will include *incubus/succubus*?

Instead of trying to find names of cities that begin with all the letters of the alphabet, try to find those that end with them. It should take some time to proceed from *Atlanta to Lodz.*

For those with more than one language, a list can be made of words of the second language that spell English words but have no connection at all with them. For example, in German: *bald, die, fast, fort, gut, hat, muss, rot, singe, wart*; in French: *à, car, main, on, or, plain, pour, sale, ton*; for Latin: *acre, age, cur, male, mane, mare, pace, possum, tale, time, violet.* There must be no etymological connection and no similar meaning.

Make up a sentence in which all the letters of the alphabet occur in alphabetical order, using as few words as possible, for example: "*A black doe fighting a jackal monopoly? 'Queer stunt,' vows foxy Zoe.*" The hunt must be for "efficient" words, such as *fighting,* which provides four letters in succession, *f, g, h, i. Monopoly* does the same. *Waxy* would come in handy.

We have many words in which the reversal of the last two letters gives an entirely different word: *fats/fast* is a good one to start with; *minute/minuet; fife/fief;* and for the metrically minded, *steer/stere.*

A word may "blend" two words such as *smog* (smoke and fog), *brunch* (breakfast and lunch). *Splotch* may be for *spot* and *blot. Twirl* is *twist* and *whirl.* A fairly new one is *cremains* for *cremated remains.* Lewis Carroll in "Jabberwocky" made up some; *chortle* (chuckle and snort), for example. This word has taken its place in our ordinary vocabulary.

Inventions are possible. Already at hand are *mathemaddicts* and *infanticipating.* No letters may be altered in either word of the pairs. A favorable review of a book may be a *complimention;* an indifferent bit of pastry, *mundanish;* a shopping spree, a *squanderlust.* George Bernard Shaw is said to have described someone as *unctimonious.* One who counts the calories can be a *gourmetric.* We have suggested some ways to relieve a *tarduous* wait.

46
Try Ya Hand at Slurvian

Slurvian is a coined word for the sloppy speech so common today (as it always has been, of course). I will be the first to confess to the regular use of *gonna*. I'm gonna admit it and state that nearly everybody uses it all the time.

A dictionary of Slurvian can be compiled simply by listening. The following specimens might start it:

censer Yuma:	Ya gotta have one.
form:	I got a messuch form.
fort:	Hurry up! H's waitin' fort.
frowers:	The fragrance lasts frowers.
laze:	Good evening, laze 'n' gemmun.
Ongana:	"Ongona sit right down and write myself a letter."
Shoonta:	He shoonta done that.
Tomb:	Give it tomb right away.
Wockin:	"Wockin I say, dear, after I say, 'I'm sorry'?"
Wowil:	I missed the plane. Wowil I do now?
Yurp:	It'ly's in Yurp.

Conclusion: Living Language

As long as a language is spoken by living people, it will undergo changes. English has certainly changed since the time of Chaucer and Shakespeare, but it has lost nothing of its vigor and versatility.

Most of the alarm being sounded today arises from misuse. But misuse generally involves sloppy structure and imprecise meaning. These do not affect the *fundamental* structure of the language. So we must define what we mean by "change." If we mean a change in the ability of the public to be precise about meanings, then we have much to worry about.

It is decidedly worthwhile to differentiate between *infer* and *imply*. What you *infer* is what you make out of what someone says. If he wants you to do that, he will try to *imply* it by what he says. "Am I to *infer* that you disagree?" "Yes, that is what my remarks *implied*." One does well to distinguish among *apt, likely,* and *liable*. Old ladies are *apt* (have a tendency) to overestimate their strength. Therefore, they are more *likely* (a matter of probability) to have accidents. If they break an expensive vase, they may be *liable* (legally responsible) for damages.

We are exasperated when we read that a tennis player "took a hiatus" from the game, or that "today's market is highly opportunistic for municipal bonds." What is happening to English is not a change in the language itself, rather the untutored tangling of misunderstood words. We have ineptitude and lack of training in rhetoric.

All the same, everyone who cares about beauty, simplicity, precision, and the delights of style must resist the slovens and deplore the pompous. See to it that people just plain "do their duty" instead of "implementing their obligations," and direct that they just plain "teach" instead of "practice strategies in a classroom situation."

Language is our principal way of communicating with one another, and communication is the heart of our very existence. Language is a magnificent accomplishment, setting us far apart from other animals. Therefore, careful attention to all it offers is of first importance, and a study of it as a phenomenon is eminently worth our while. Listen to it, reflect upon its astounding possibilities, strive for a clear style and precise utterance, reflect upon its amazing creation by humans, aim for its integrity.

Bibliography

Books

American Heritage Dictionary. Boston: Houghton Mifflin, 1976.

Bernstein, Theodore M. *The Careful Writer.* New York: Atheneum, 1965.

Bremner, John B. *Words on Words.* New York: Columbia University Press, 1980.

Busnel, R. G. II, and Classe, A. *Whistled Languages.* New York: Springer-Verlag, 1976.

Campbell, Hannah. *Why Did They Name It . . . ?* New York: Bell Publishing, 1964.

Carrington, John F. *Talking Drums of Africa.* London: Carey Kingsgate Press, 1949; New York: Negro Universities Press, 1969.

Clark, Virginia P., Eschholz, Paul A., and Rosa, Alfred F., eds. *Language: Introductory Readings.* New York: St. Martin's Press, 1977.

Copperud, Roy H. *American Usage and Style: The Consensus.* New York: Van Nostrand Reinhold, 1979.

Francis, W. Nelson. *The Structure of American English.* New York: Ronald Press, 1958.

Friedman, Lynn A. *On the Other Hand.* New York: Academic Press, 1977.

Grambs, David. *Words about Words.* New York: McGraw-Hill, 1984.

Hall, Edward T. *The Silent Language.* New York: Doubleday, 1973.

Jespersen, Otto. *Essentials of English Grammar.* Tuscaloosa: University of Alabama Press, 1964.

Klima, Edward S., and Bellugi, Ursula. *The Signs of Language.* Cambridge: Harvard University Press, 1979.

Kurath, Hans. *A Word Geography of the Eastern United States.* Ann Arbor: University of Michigan Press, 1949.

Lipton, James. *An Exaltation of Larks.* New York: Grossman, 1968.

Moore, John Cecil. *You English Words.* Philadelphia: Lippincott, 1962.

Murray, K. M. Elizabeth. *Caught in the Web of Words.* New Haven: Yale University Press, 1977.

Partridge, Eric. *A Dictionary of Slang and Unconventional Usage.* New York: Macmillan, 1970.

Pike, Kenneth L. *The Intonation of American English.* Ann Arbor: University of Michigan Press, 1979.

Rawson, Hugh. *A Dictionary of Euphemisms and Other Doubletalk.* New York: Crown, 1981.

Schur, Norman W. *English English.* Essex, Conn.: A Verbatim Book, 1973, 1980.

Zinsser, William K. *On Writing Well.* New York: Harper & Row, 1980.

Webster's Third New International Dictionary of the English Language, unabridged. Springfield: G. & C. Merriam, 1968.

Periodicals

American Speech, Tuscaloosa: University of Alabama Press, 1926–.

Verbatim. Laurence Urdang, Box 668, Essex, Conn. 06246, 1974–.

Word Ways. A. Ross Eckler, Spring Valley Road, Morristown, N.J. 07960, 1968–.